A Hope-Filled Journey
Under His Sky

A Hope-Filled Journey
Under His Sky

Bruce G. Allder

RESOURCE *Publications* • Eugene, Oregon

A HOPE-FILLED JOURNEY UNDER HIS SKY

Copyright © 2016 Bruce G. Allder. All rights reserved. Except for brief quotations in critical publications or reviews, no part of this book may be reproduced in any manner without prior written permission from the publisher. Write: Permissions, Wipf and Stock Publishers, 199 W. 8th Ave., Suite 3, Eugene, OR 97401.

Resource Publications
An Imprint of Wipf and Stock Publishers
199 W. 8th Ave., Suite 3
Eugene, OR 97401

www.wipfandstock.com

PAPERBACK ISBN: 978-1-4982-9671-7
HARDCOVER ISBN: 978-1-4982-9673-1
EBOOK ISBN: 978-1-4982-9672-4

Manufactured in the U.S.A.   OCTOBER 26, 2016

Contents

Preface | vii
Brief Biographical Overview | ix

Chapter 1	Responses in the Cancer Journey	1
Chapter 2	The Calling	14
Chapter 3	The Missionary	33
Chapter 4	Doing Life	64
Chapter 5	The Medical Journey	79
Chapter 6	The Family Journey	102
Chapter 7	Faith Reflections	117

Preface

AT 8 A.M. WEDNESDAY, February 15, 2012, our precious, dynamic, missionary daughter Belinda, known to many as BJ, slipped from this world into the next, at the age of thirty-three years. Her two-and-a-half year battle with cancer was over. Far from a sense of defeat, she left with an air of triumph and grace. As she was taking her last breath after two days of unconsciousness, she turned her head toward Jacque (my wife) and her best friend Melinda (Mel) and smiled. The smile stayed on her face in death. It was like her final "thank you" to two very special people and an acknowledgment that where she was going was all that she had hoped for.

It is my intention in these next pages to celebrate the life of BJ. It is also a very personal journey for Jacque and me as we try and put words to thoughts and feelings that sometimes appear too deep to articulate. Our grief for our daughter has been deep and painful, despite the graceful way in which she prepared for her ultimate passing. I am thankful to have been given a semester sabbatical leave from my assignment at Nazarene Theological College, Brisbane, to have the space to work through many of the emotions and thoughts that have bombarded me these past few months.

I do not take this journey alone. Jacque, my best friend, lover, and wife of over thirty-nine years, shares these difficult days with me. Together we have worked through BJ's diaries, her written assignments from her studies, and the many statements of support and encouragement that have come from our many friends around the world. While these are my words, the journey is shared with Jacque. This is a walk that I would not have wanted to take without her. She has brought much needed strength and balance as we have cried together, laughed together and been surprised together at God's amazing grace. Our two boys, Tim and Mitch, along with their wives, Carine and Mariko, have been an important part of this journey. My parents and Jacque's mum have also walked much of this road with us as well.

Preface

In addition to the celebration of BJ's life, I also share some of the principles that BJ established in her life and work as a missionary. I encounter these principles through her journey, often expressed in her own words recorded for us in her diaries, papers written toward her master of arts, which was awarded posthumously, various interviews of BJ, written comments by those involved in various aspects of her life and ministry, along with many informal conversations that Jacque and I had with BJ the last two and a half years together. Where possible I let BJ "speak," hence you will see extensive quotes from her writings.

Interspersed between accounts of BJ's activities and thoughts are my own in an effort to illustrate the principles that guided her activity. The principles are only briefly mentioned and my brief comments on them do not do them full justice. It is hoped they may at least spark further thinking and reflection. We understand that those who have suffered similarly may have a completely different journey. But whatever the path we each take, we thank God for his tender love that is sustaining us. We continue to walk the road of life, conscious of God's grace in our lives, even if we do so now with a profound sense of loss.

Bruce G. Allder

Brief Biographical Overview

- May 4, 1978: Belinda Jacque Allder born to Bruce and Jacque Allder in Brisbane, Australia.
- November 19, 1980: Birth of brother Tim.
- January 1984–June 1986: Travelled to United States with family for Bruce to attend Nazarene Theological Seminary.
- January 1984: Started school in Olathe, Kansas.
- June 1986: Returned to Sydney.
- 1986–1989: Attended Regents Park State Primary School.
- 1990–1995: Attended Sefton State High School as "selective" student (acceptance based upon high academic performance at primary school and entrance exam).
- September 4, 1992: Birth of brother Mitch.
- 1996–1999: Attended University of Western Sydney (UWS).
- June 1998: Youth in Mission trip to Fiji, heard call to serve God "under his sky."
- December 1998: Graduated with bachelor of teaching degree.
- January 1999–June 2000: Worked as primary school teacher (year 2 students) at Greenacre Christian Community School.
- December 1999: Graduated with bachelor of education in creative arts.
- 2001: Overseas teaching experience in London, with best friend Mel.
- 2002: Volunteer English teacher at Maetang Tribal Children's Home, Thailand.
- 2002–September 2009: Missionary work in northern Thailand.

Brief Biographical Overview

- September 2009: Home assignment.
- October 2009: Diagnosed with stage 4 cancer.
- November 2010: Awarded TESOL Certificate IV from New Horizons School of English (first student to graduate from this school of English, which is a department of Nazarene Theological College, Brisbane).
- December 2010: Visited Thailand for two weeks, in between chemo sessions.
- November 2011: Successfully completed course work for master of arts from NTC.
- January 2012: Final visit, for 5 days, to Thailand for opening activities of 3rd Wave Youth Leadership conference in Bangkok.
- January 16, 2012: Told by oncologist that cancer could no longer be treated with chemo. It was time to return home and enjoy the rest of her time with family and friends.
- January 18, 2012: Commenced home-based palliative care.
- February 9, 2012: Awarded "Good Samaritan Award" from Church of the Nazarene by Rev. David Harris, NCM coordinator, Asia Pacific Region, and Rev. Dr. John Moore, FSC, Australia and New Zealand.
- February 9, 2012: Final family Communion service.
- February 15, 2012: Passed away at home, 8 a.m.

Chapter 1

Responses in the Cancer Journey

THE JOURNEY THROUGH EXTENDED terminal illness for both the afflicted person and their family is, in one sense, a very lonely one. This was our pathway as a family and there were very few in our circle of friends who could really identify with us. There was no shortage of well-meaning advice given, books passed on to read, and anecdotes of people who had beaten the insidious disease of cancer. There were times when we would have loved to have not heard the perennial question "How is BJ doing?" Perhaps that was part of our denial, but the questions were a constant reminder of the relentless challenge facing BJ. Were the constant queries superficial? Sometimes it felt like it. Whether or not this was the case, their questions prompted more profound soul-searching questions for us as a family. Is it possible that BJ can beat this disease? How long will we have her with us? Where is God in this?

BJ journaled, and soon after her diagnosis of cancer, she began a "Thank You" diary. Each day she wrote something for which to thank God. This was a very personal diary that she only allowed the family to read a few days prior to her death. As I read the diary, knowing the context in which many of the comments were made, I was both humbled and amazed at the grace and wisdom expressed. Her words challenged me in my walk with Jesus and I marvel at the insight and love expressed. There are many comments about "doing life" and it is from this diary that much of the material that follows has been gleaned.

In the preface to her 2010 journal, BJ quoted from *Surviving Cancer*:

> When we have been diagnosed with a life threatening illness, when we have had the bone pointed at us, we have a very clear choice to make—to spend our remaining time living, or to spend it dying, to live each day to the full, or wait to die. But we do not need that

prognosis. Every moment of our lives we all have that choice—to spend that moment living, to spend it dying.[1]

She then wrote, "*I choose living!!*" Her choice was clear!

The two and a half years of living in Brisbane for treatment were filled with ministry opportunities for BJ. In a video update sent to ministry colleagues in Thailand some ten months into her chemotherapy, she outlined the choices she faced and her decision to be active.

> I can't believe it has been over twelve months since I saw you last. So much has happened in that twelve months. I am sure you can see that I am a bit fatter, less hair. Twelve months of chemo later . . . I thank you for journeying with me through this time—your prayers and encouragement and support has been such a blessing to me. He has really helped me through this time. And those prayers are really healing me. I really do believe that. An update on what is happening with me. The cancer in my body still continues to shrink. All of my results show that. It has been a longer process than I had anticipated, but it is all in God's timing. My lung is now clear, and my bowel is now operable. But before they can do that the liver has to have some more work. It is still too covered (with cancer) and so we are still working on shrinking it on the liver. So I just ask for your prayers that that will happen and then move on to the next process of having operations on that.
>
> Like I said, this twelve months has been an amazing journey. I praise God for having good health—as much as I have. I have been able to do so much. *One of the decisions I had to work through was to be here and to enjoy being here rather than feeling like a visitor or laying around sick. And so I have just tried to be involved as much as I can—wherever God wants*, studying here at college, and I completed my teaching English certificate, and participated in teaching in the free English at the English School here. It has been a fun time of new adventures and God really has taught me a lot.
>
> I thank you for journeying with me through this. I hope to keep you updated and hope to see you all really really soon![2]

The Holiness campaign began tonight. It was a blessing to lead worship tonight and have Mel sing with me again. Nice![3]

---

1. Paul Kraus, *Surviving Cancer* (Adelaide: Griffin, 2008), 194.
2. BJ Allder, video greeting sent to colleagues in Thailand, Dec 2010, emphasis mine.
3. BJ Allder, unpublished diary, Aug 25, 2010 (hereafter, "BJ diary"), emphasis mine.

Thank you God for being able to have a full day with Him!! Spoke at Capalaba Church of the Nazarene this morning. It was a sending service for the PNG Work & Witness team. Great! Glad to be asked to be involved in stuff like that. YIM team to Maryborough meeting this afternoon—great! I'm excited to be involved in something like that and exciting to see others get involved too! Had great chat with Belinda Jeffs.[4]

BJ's decision to choose to "enjoy life" was not a self-centred one. Her desire to participate in what God is doing in his world and especially with people shone through! Her choice to live and enjoy life really meant a choice to "live" for others. Ultimately this choice wasn't about BJ. It was a door to a continued and amazing impact she has had around the world. Neither was this decision taken lightly. It was one of great courage and faith. It led to making daily choices to be disciplined in being outwardly focussed, consistently participating in times of worship (both privately and in groups) and in service of others.

This journey is mirrored in Psalm 77:

> I cried out to God for help; I cried out to God to hear me. When I was in distress, I sought the Lord; at night I stretched out untiring hands and my soul refused to be comforted. I remembered you, O God, and I groaned; I mused, and my spirit grew faint. (Ps 77:1–3 NIV)

Here there is a cry of anguish at suffering and trouble along with the plea for help directed to the Lord. The distress in this psalm appears to be personal rather than a national distress. In BJ's case this personal distress was not just the news of cancer, but a rapid deterioration in her physical condition until the doctors could find medication to slow the progress of this insidious disease. Until doctors could bring the increasing pain under control, as parents, we also were traumatised watching BJ lie in the foetal position, weeping in pain. This does something to a parent that is hard to describe. The words "I cried out to the Lord" seem so lame to describe what we were feeling. We cried out to the Lord with what Dennis Apple, in his book *Life After the Death of My Son*, describes as the primordial cry of pain that only a parent losing a child utters. We would trade places with her; we would take her illness for her; we would give her our lives in order to see her live without pain. Oh, yes, we identify with the cry of the anguished heart! We lived some of these psalms! (Pss 6, 22, 38, 41, 88, 102):

4. BJ diary, Sept 19, 2010.

> You kept my eyes from closing; I was too troubled to speak. I thought about the former days, the years of long ago; I remembered my songs in the night. My heart mused and my spirit inquired: "Will the Lord reject forever? Will he never show his favour again? Has his unfailing love vanished forever? Has his promise failed for all time? Has God forgotten to be merciful? Has he in anger withheld his compassion?" (Ps 77:4–9 NIV)

Here is the anguish of suffering. The feelings of abandonment to the point of wondering whether God even cares, are expressed with a depth of pathos that is gut wrenching. If it were the number of prayers given with great earnestness that determined whether God would answer, BJ would indeed have been healed! Several prayer chains were organised. People overseas, who did not even know BJ personally, created a prayer quilt for her with many "loose" threads that indicated prayers spoken on her behalf. The international church was mobilised to pray. BJ was overwhelmed and humbled by the outpouring of prayer for her around the world.

She loved the Psalms that could express her (and our) anguish and pain so well. It is important to note, though, that BJ, in her anguish, never questioned God. This, for us, was an amazing grace. We had questions—but she didn't!

> Everyone's like, "How'd you feel? Did you get angry?" No, from the beginning there was just a peace that God's in control and there was just a peace about it. I didn't ever question God once, and I still don't. I believe that God can heal me, but I also know that He may not and that is His plan. Even up until now, in these last few days, I can see how He's using my story; that there is a hope and my life can continue to be used. That's my prayer each day right now.[5]

Psalm 77 continues:

> Then I thought, "To this I will appeal: the years of the right hand of the Most High." I will remember the deeds of the Lord; yes, I will remember your miracles of long ago. I will meditate on all your works and consider all your mighty deeds (Ps 77:10–12 NIV).

There is a change of focus by the psalmist in these next verses. The psalmist makes a decision: *I will remember* the deeds of the Lord (v. 11); *I will meditate* on your works (v. 12).

---

5. Belinda Allder, "Under His Sky," *Engage*, Feb 6, 2012, http://www.engagemagazine.com/content/under-his-sky-belinda-allders-story.

> Your ways, O God, are holy. What god is so great as our God? You are the God who performs miracles; you display your power among the people. With your mighty arm you redeemed your people, the descendants of Jacob and Joseph. (Ps 77:13–15 NIV)

Now there is a whole different atmosphere as a result of the psalmist's change of focus. Despite the circumstances in which the psalmist finds himself, after turning his attention to God, he recognises God's holiness, his miraculous deeds, and redemption for his people. A sense of hope is found. This is what gave BJ the courage to "choose to live" the last few months of her life, rather than spend them dying.

Hope is what characterised Belinda's ministry but particularly the journey through her illness.

> Watched Loiue Giglio's *Fruitcake and Ice Cream* DVD. What a challenge! A challenge to always be sharing Jesus Christ with others! Evangelism stuff is hitting me from all angles at the moment—reflecting on camp / youth, evangelism class, evangelism paper, Bible study tonight etc. etc. . . . Lord continue to speak to me and guide me. May I be fruitcake!![6]

> Hope! Watched Loiue Giglio DVD for Bible Study on hope in trouble. It was great! Don't know what else to write here except thanks, God, for the girls. Love that message and most of all thanks, God, for being my HOPE!! (my "anchor" and may I be a "megaphone" for your glory!)[7]

> Jesus! How could I not be thankful for Jesus on Christmas Day! Without Him where would we be? Life would have no meaning. There would be no *hope, peace, joy & love*. I am truly grateful for all of these. I have experienced all of these in a new way this year. Thank you Lord, for these amazing gifts.[8]

> The HOPE we have in Him! The promise of eternal life. Went to a funeral today—made me think of what my funeral may be like—it is sad, yet so happy as we reflect on someone's life and God's goodness and faithfulness and then to think of the eternal future

---

6. BJ diary, Aug 10, 2010.
7. Ibid., Aug 24, 2010.
8. Ibid., Dec 25, 2010.

with Him—and have it so much better than life here—no pain, no tears! Thanx God![9]

A day considering Buddhism in World Religions class. It is really good to consider it. Wow!! I am so thankful for the HOPE we have in Jesus Christ . . . and in just knowing there is a God! I am also so thankful for one life . . . it is not a past life that has given me cancer.[10]

Christmas! Thank you Lord for all that Christmas is!!! Thank you for sending your Son to the world for us. Thank you for the HOPE that that brings to us all. I live in that HOPE. You came, You died for me!!! That I might live forever with you! That is the HOPE that I cling to now. I thank you that you bring meaning and direction to our lives. Without that I don't know what I would be doing during all of this. I thank you that I have seen another Christmas—and what a family time it was—29 of us for Christmas lunch! It was lovely!! Still not feeling 100% but getting there—was able to lead worship this morning. Thank you for the many blessings—that is Christmas presents that I received—wow! So lucky! And a star named after me!—Wow![11]

Psalm 77 concludes:

The waters saw you, O God, the water saw you and writhed; the very depths were convulsed. The clouds poured down water, the skies resounded with thunder; your arrows flashed back and forth. Your thunder was heard in the whirlwind, your lightning lit up the world; the earth trembled and quaked. Your path led through the sea, your way through the mighty waters, though your footprints were not seen. You led your people like a flock by the hand of Moses and Aaron. (Ps 77:16–20 NIV)

The challenge here is that the psalmist goes on to describe continued difficulty and trauma. The subtle change of structure in the psalm in vv. 16–17 seem to emphasise the continuing trauma. There was no apparent respite from the difficulties facing the psalmist. The decision did not change the circumstances. However, the trauma is faced with a sense of

9. Ibid., May 6, 2011.
10. Ibid., July 20, 2011.
11. Ibid., Dec 25, 2011. The star coordinates are given in the International Star Registry—Crux RA 12h 42m 52s D-62 15. The name of the star is "BJ's Star: Under His Sky Forever."

hope because of declaration of God's presence and power in the midst of the difficulty.

> Your path led through the sea, your ways through the mighty waters, though your footprints were not seen. (v. 19)

This was BJ's experience. She was glad for a Bible that expressed her anguish, but at the end of the day, pointed to a hope in a God who would be with her in the midst of the storm. She couldn't always see God at work in the midst of all that was going on, but BJ relentlessly hung onto a hope in her God.

> Psalm 13 has been speaking to me a lot this past week when I have felt so blah! I made my Facebook status "living in Ps 13"—because that's the truth!
>
>> How long, O Lord? Will you forget me forever? How long will you hide your face from me? How long must I bear pain in my soul, and have sorrow in my heart all day long? How long shall my enemy be exalted over me? Consider and answer me, O Lord my God! Give light to my eyes, or I will sleep the sleep of death, And my enemy will say, "I have prevailed"; My foes will rejoice because I am shaken. But I trust in your steadfast love; My heart shall rejoice in your salvation. I will sing to the Lord, because he has dealt bountifully with me. (Psalm 13 NRSV)
>
> I've studied this psalm before but this is the first time it has just called out to me and meant so much more. I thank God for David and his writings that are just so real—so how I feel! This is I guess the first time my cancer has just got to me and got me feeling down—as well as other stuff going on. But as I cry out like David did at the beginning of the Psalm, I can pause and wait . . . and really mean vs 5 & 6. Despite of everything I trust in His unfailing love!!! (Some days it is hard to say . . . but it is there!)[12]

The decision to trust God, no matter the circumstances, was no easy one to make, nor one with which to live. On the title page of her 2010 diary BJ had written, "Greater things have yet to come . . . greater things are still to be done." This is a quote from the song made popular by one of BJ's favourite artists, Chris Tomlin.

The story behind the writing of this song so captured BJ that this became her theme song for the first eighteen months she was home. Aaron Boyd of Bluetree, a contemporary Christian band, tells of the time that his

---

12. BJ diary, June 14, 2011.

pastor asked that music group to make a mission trip to Pattaya, Thailand. Through a whole series of people connecting with people, an invitation was given to Aaron Boyd and his group to perform a two-hour music set in a bar in Pattaya. He describes the bar as more of a brothel than anything else and he was challenged to sing "Jesus songs" for two hours. He had no idea how he would be received, but by gathering a whole bunch of Christians to join him in the bar, buy cokes, and listen to his music, Jesus songs were heard up and down that street of bars, strip clubs and gambling dens. While singing, the words of a song, later to be called "God of This City," came to him. He saw the sin and destruction that was about him, but recognised that God was the God of this city as well. The people about that place just didn't know it. The song begins as a sombre, downbeat song in a minor key, but concludes as an anthem of God's power to save. This gripped BJ's missionary heart. She inspired many young people to see a future with God working, rather than a future that had everyone working hard on their own agenda. It was an affirmation that God was in the process of doing some amazing things if we would just open our hearts and minds to see what it is.

BJ continues:

> "Greater things . . ." Through this time God has been teaching me that He really does have a plan for me—and it's not always as I thought it would be! Let's be honest, this is NOT how I planned to spend this time and into 2010! Given a choice I would not come willingly into this . . . BUT I have seen so many positive things during this time! I have seen evidence of "greater things." I just KNOW he has me in His hands!
>
> Once I had come to terms with the fact I will be here for a while, I was challenged to get more active in some church life (Christian life with others). I spoke with Mel about the possibilities of us having a Bible study together. I mean, man! I need to take advantage of being so close (in distance) to my best friend, and also having other English speaking Christians around. Mel and I agreed we should do something like that and then I was challenged to talk to Melissa (BJ's cousin) about it. I had heard that she had gone to a Bible study in the US for a while but I have no idea of what she thought of it or why she stopped going. But anyway I felt this was the time—since I am here longer—to ask her. So I emailed her (a bit woosy, I know). I just asked her if she would be interested, but didn't want her to feel pressured. I sent the email and prayed! A couple of days later she replied. She was interested. She said she is interested in learning more and listening to other

people's opinions. A good response I thought. She also reacted as I thought she might and how I would if I was in her situation—saying it would have to be in preschool terms because she is not a pro like us . . . haha . . . cute but understandable. (She doesn't realise how not pro I really am). We decided to start something when Mel gets back from Sydney—after their Christmas / New Year trip.

I also began to think about Muz—the only other young girl (20–30s) in church. I was chatting with her on Facebook and asked her about it too—and another great response—she just opened up and telling me that's something she really needs—and to be with girls. She mainly hangs with the guys. She was also sharing that she hasn't been involved in a Bible study for a while now and it is making her spiritually dry. I can totally relate to that so it seems this is all a God thing and another way He has shown me He wants me here for now!!

"Greater things are still to be done!"[13]

BJ made an amazingly courageous decision to live life to the full despite the circumstances. However, there is something profound also going on in this preface to her journal. She begins to see the ministry opportunities before her, not as some great divine revelation, but through a gentle openness to God's leading and sensitivity to the Spirit's leading. There is something very ordinary about this, but we are so glad that she did not miss it. Its consequence was as dramatic as a "Damascus Road experience." Oh how often we miss it, though, because the leading comes within the gentle cloak of everyday life.

With a diagnosis of 4th-stage bowel cancer, BJ struggled to make Brisbane her interim home. Brisbane, and staying with Mum and Dad, was "home" for the foreseeable future. She connected with several of the local Nazarene congregations and began to give of herself in selfless ways, leading worship, mentoring youth leadership, and generally being an enthusiastic participant in worship services.

BJ wrote in her "Thank You Journal":

Church relationships growing—went and visited Uncle Tom (local church member who was terminally ill) in hospital.[14]

I want to thank God for the life of Tom Vanderslick. It was his funeral today. It was beautiful. He was a wonderful man of

13. BJ diary, preface, 2010.
14. Ibid., Apr 8, 2010.

God—always happy (despite the pain), funny, praising God, sharing Jesus, a true family man, active church family man, true man of God. Love you Tom!![15]

And yes, there were times when the local congregation recognised BJ's own needs:

There was special prayer in church today for me. It was unexpected but very much appreciated!! The church family here at Meadowlands really has become my church family. They are always so concerned and loving. It was nice to be back there today after so many weeks away.[16]

Thank you God for the Meadowlands church family. They really have been so encouraging to me through the whole journey. They are always encouraging about my leading (in worship).[17]

Encouragement from church folk! They always want to tell me what an encouragement I am to them—but that just encourages me more![18]

Additionally, BJ had connections all over the world, and her global family was an amazing support to us. Each time there was a district church function, the church would gather to pray for BJ. Many around the world kept in regular contact with her through Skype, e-mail, texts . . .

Engage Magazine: How has the church embraced you during all of this?

BJ: Oh, the church has been awesome, I mean globally. Especially in these last few weeks, I am just so humbled by how much support. For the whole two and a half years, my family around the world has just been so supportive and prayed constantly, and that's really, really held me up.

The thing is, people say, "Oh you're so strong," or whatever. It's not me; it's the support that keeps me going and holds me up really. And so the church has really been my strength. And it's been awesome because it's also been a witness to those non-Christians

---

15. Ibid., Apr 23, 2010.
16. Ibid., Jan 23, 2011.
17. Ibid., Sept 15, 2011.
18. Ibid., Dec 4, 2011.

around because they can see it and they're just like, "Wow. You have so much support."[19]

There were other expressions of support. My ministry colleague at NTC, David McEwan, connected with us at significant moments of the journey. A sympathetic hand on the shoulder, a passage of Scripture read or a prayer together helped us find an anchor for our souls. It was David McEwan who was there to pray with me when we had first heard of the cancer diagnosis. He was present in the last days to administer the Lord's Supper to us as a family—the last time that we were all present as a family with BJ. He was at BJ's bedside immediately after her passing to read Scripture and pray with us as a family. Without these times of bringing the Word of God to us, I am not sure what we would have done. We were too numb to do some of these things for ourselves.

> Thank you God for the community of faith! Today I was anointed with oil for healing. The elders and college community prayed over me in chapel. It was a very special time led by Richard. I am thankful for a Christian community who is believing in faith with me that I will be healed.[20]

A further amazing expression of support for us as a family came from outside the church through Jacque's work colleagues at the Thornlands State School. Jacque has worked there as a teacher aide in special education for over eighteen years. They had "passed the hat" around and raised in excess of $800 toward BJ's expenses as well as provided vouchers for meals out, lawn mowing, haircuts, etc. Additionally, while BJ was still active, the school hosted "The Biggest Morning Tea" fund-raising event for cancer research, as well as participated in other cancer research fund-raisers like "Daffodil Day."

> Thank you God for the support I get through my cancer journey! The "Biggest Morning Tea" at Mum's school was so nice—nice to see Mum so supported too!! I got to draw the winning ticket ☺.[21]

In the last week or so of BJ's life, work colleagues would drop in around morning tea time each day with freshly brewed coffee; spend a few minutes giving encouraging words, and move on to the rest of their day. I

---

19. Belinda Allder, "Under His Sky," *Engage*, Feb 6, 2012.
20. BJ diary, Aug 25, 2010.
21. Ibid., May 25, 2011.

was thrilled for Jacque that such support was evident (even though Jacque had taken unpaid leave from her job for a whole school term) and I know BJ, when conscious, expressed her appreciation of their thoughtfulness.

Another powerful and practical expression of support came from a Nazarene congregation in Brisbane. Even though we do not attend this particular congregation, the Logan Community Church of the Nazarene brought in meals every day for a week after BJ's passing. This meant we did not have to worry about food preparation through a very difficult period when even routine things sapped what little energy we had. What an amazing ministry! What a sacrificial service to those of us in need. This was a source of encouragement to us; a reminder that there were those around us who were prepared to help carry the load. We had nursed BJ at home, and the last week of her life particularly, had left us exhausted, physically and emotionally. I gained a whole new appreciation for those who care for loved ones 24/7. Sleep patterns remained disrupted for weeks afterwards and the sense of extreme tiredness lingered for months.

One of the greatest challenges of BJ's life is her example of seeing the ministry opportunities wherever she was planted for the moment. There was no spectacular vision of what she ought to do; no bolt of lightning to jar her into a new direction. Rather this sensitivity was a result of being in tune with gentle promptings of God's Spirit. As she discussed with her best friend, Mel, the idea of having a Bible study together, her cousin and the young lady at church came to mind as well. She acted on those promptings, as ordinary as they may have appeared to be. But it all started with her decision to choose living, not dying—to bloom where she was planted, in spite of the difficult circumstances.

BJ was never about the big and flashy: it was about saying "yes" to Jesus. *It was about walking slowly among the people.*[22]

> Ah, the joy that she brought into every gathering, whether official or otherwise. I have never worked with a more effective missionary, and Thailand is so much richer for having her life lived before both young and old alike. Her footprints will be seen there for many years to come, and she has left behind many disciples for the Kingdom. Well done, BJ![23]

---

22. Rolf Kleinfeldt, "Under His Sky," Facebook page, accessed Feb 15, 2012, http://www.facebook.com/UnderHisSky.

23. Michael McCarty, "Under His Sky" Facebook page, accessed Feb, 2012.

> Lifestyle evangelism. Really not that hard when we are fully plugged into Him! My life is one of the most powerful tools of evangelism I can use right now. I need to recharge and be fully plugged into Him![24]

It was the *walking slowly among the people* that made her that *effective missionary*. She just did life with people and became that authentic disciple of Jesus that was believable by those around her. She showed that walking with Jesus was a natural part of living; nothing super-spiritual, no pretence—just a commitment to walking the journey with as many people as possible. It was this perspective in "doing life" that BJ brought to her journey with cancer.

> Blessed are those whose strength is in you, who have set their hearts on pilgrimage. As they pass through the Valley of Bacca, they make it a place of springs. (Ps 84:5–6 NIV)

---

24. BJ diary, Jan 24, 2003.

Chapter 2

The Calling

It is clear that BJ lived with a "calling" on her life. Throughout her growing up years there were a number of experiences that acted as signposts to that calling. God was preparing a very special missionary.

From the age of two, BJ wanted to be a teacher. We are not sure what started the interest, but while living in unit 4 at Nazarene Theological College as a toddler, she would eagerly watch for the older children returning home from school. As soon as she saw them she would want to spend time with them, watch them do their homework, and pretend to be doing homework as well. She loved to play school with these older children. When no one was around to play, she would line up all her soft toys and have them as students in her "classroom." Jacque would read stories to her every day, and often several times a day. BJ quickly developed the love of reading. It was not unusual to see BJ engrossed in a book. One time she fell down the stairs of our town house in the United States because she was reading a book and not watching for the stairs. At another time she had been told to go to sleep, but Jacque found her very late at night with her head under the bedcovers continuing to read by torch light so as not to disturb anyone (or get caught staying up too late!).

BJ loved to talk! As soon as she began learning to form words as a toddler, she began using phrases, and not just isolated words. She was like a sponge, soaking up new words and looking for any opportunity to try out the newly discovered words. Tim, our older son and two years her junior, was slow to develop speech. We were concerned enough to take him to a speech pathologist, but we were assured that there was no physiological impediment to his speaking. As time went on we discovered that he would just rely on BJ to do the talking for him. He was content to let BJ take the lead, and on many occasions, have her speak for him. Put Tim by himself and he was articulate and engaged as any toddler his age.

Over the years we have seen this "habit" continue. Tim developed the skill and desire to work behind the scenes on activities. He became the sound man at church and whenever BJ had special functions to organise during her two and a half years in Brisbane, Tim would provide technical support in sound and lighting. They have been close as brother and sister, and I think that Tim was more than happy to operate the sound levels when BJ was talking. He felt he had ultimate control by being able to turn her down (or off!!) when he thought she was going on too much.

One day BJ came home from high school devastated that her career guidance officer advised against her becoming a teacher. "There would be no jobs," she apparently said. We were more than happy for Belinda to prepare to do something else, but thankfully we encouraged her to follow her heart. We had several conversations about how God would lead her and that she ought to listen to God in making the choice. In all of that, she still could not conceive of being anything other than a teacher. So, after successfully completing high school, she enrolled in a dual degree in teaching and education at the University of Western Sydney. It was on her first day at university that BJ met Melinda, who became her closest and dearest friend. They clicked straight away, and it wasn't long before BJ introduced Mel to her "other best friend," Jesus. Mel continues to have a vital relationship with Jesus, and is about sharing her faith with those around her.

BJ's experiences through primary and high schools were positive. She was an excellent student and missed being dux (top student) of the primary school by just one mark. However, she was school captain the last year of primary school, very popular with school friends, and developed effective leadership skills. BJ was accepted into a nearby high school that specialised in higher achieving students. When studying alongside other good students, she continued to develop well, both academically and socially. It was clear from the outset that her best subjects and interest lay in the arts, not the sciences. BJ became an accomplished flautist, participating in school bands and musicals. She wanted to be in everything! She excelled at sports such as netball, hockey, basketball and touch football. One of her highlights was playing in the school orchestra at the Sydney Opera House! All the sports she enjoyed were team sports, which developed her strong team spirit and her desire to engage with people. It was apparent that it was the social interaction of the sports that appealed to her the most. The positive educational experiences just whetted her appetite to be more involved in teaching and in people's lives.

We did notice an interesting, and initially for us, a worrying trend at university. Her grades were solidly average and just above average. We knew she was a good student if she applied herself, and we were not sure of her diligence in study. She was busy in youth group activities at church and we were unsure whether she was devoting enough time to the studies. In typical fashion, BJ studied "best" lying on her bedroom floor (despite having a nice desk!) surrounded by books and all kinds of paraphernalia, chatting on the phone and listening to music. It was toward the end of her university studies that she understood herself enough to explain her average grades to us. She did not want to excel and leave her friends behind. Her good friends at university were also bright students so I suspect that they all thought the same way and were happy with moderate grades to ensure an active social life! Once again, her people focus shone through.

BJ testified to meeting Jesus in a personal way at a children's camp when she was eight. She never went through the "terrible teens," or rebelled against authority, or sought to experiment with destructive things such as alcohol or drugs. I attribute that to a real, growing relationship with Jesus through those teen years and being involved in a church that was fun. However, Jacque and I remember a few occasions (mostly the latter portion of our time in the United States) when BJ began to exert newfound independence and tested the boundaries. This was well and truly before her teen years. We wondered, while as a preteen she pushed boundaries, what she would be like as a rebellious teenager! We thank the Lord that these attitudes were dealt with early! Her assertion did reveal, though, a strong will and resiliency which benefited her later. Jacque and I are probably like most parents—we didn't really know what we were doing raising children. We just took each issue as it came and asked the Lord to help us do the right thing. Nevertheless, it was BJ's finding a childlike faith in Jesus Christ that put her on the road to serving Jesus and others in such an effective way.

This relationship with Jesus provided the opportunity to establish a secure identity. BJ's bright bubbly personality was a reflection of being comfortable in who she was as a child of God. She exuded a quiet confidence in herself that was never arrogant. Certainly as parents we did our best to convey to each of our children that they could be and do anything that they put their mind, heart and energies into. It appeared that BJ was comfortable in her own skin.

Belinda grew up in a very positive church context. Reflecting back on our days at Birrong Church of the Nazarene, Sydney (1986–99), I realised that congregation got community living right. The congregation, made up of many senior adults, young people of high school age, and young adults, learned to support each other and do life together. While I was the lead pastor, David Harris, my long-term associate and colleague in ministry, displayed a gift in leading people in doing life together. Hospitality, the inclusive spirit of embracing the stranger, multiculturalism expressed through a coming together of a multitude of different cultures, and the celebration of diversity, were all features of that congregation through the 1990s. This was the norm for BJ and she took this with her into her own ministry contexts.

Rev. Ian Lowther was a member of the Birrong ministry team with a focus on prayer and visitation. He was a deeply spiritual man who exuded a love for people and a caring heart for others that was exemplary. During his time at Birrong he was diagnosed with cancer. He allowed the church people to journey with him through those difficult days until his death. His transparency and tenacious faith were an inspiration. He taught us much about walking through life with a terminal medical condition and yet keeping a focus on Jesus. Toward the end of his cancer journey the congregation hired two busses and travelled across to the retirement village in which he lived with his wife, and gathered in a community room. His wife wheeled him into the room and for the next forty-five minutes we sang, prayed and worshipped together. While Ian was in pain, he still had a radiant smile, a glowing testimony to God's goodness and thankful for a community of believers who shared in worship together. I have often wondered whether Ian Lowther's example formed the context for BJ's response to her own illness.

Rev. David Harris, my dear friend and ministry colleague from Birrong days, changed his ministry assignment after we left Sydney (for Brisbane and Nazarene Theological College) but continued to be BJ's pastor wherever she was in the world. This pastoral connection was invaluable. During BJ's illness, David would occasionally fly to Brisbane from Sydney at his own expense to spend a couple of days with BJ and the family. He would simply "hang out" with us and above all else showed he cared.

> I thank God for Dave (Harris)—my second Dad, my mentor, my friend! I thank God for having him in my life. He came up today (Friday) just to spend the whole weekend with me. So super special and so exciting!! I feel so much better today and I know it is from having amazing people to hang out with—it blesses me and refreshes me. I thank you Lord for the love and care of his family to me and how much they are family to me and that will never

change. I thank God for the time we were actually able to work together again this arvo (afternoon) as we prepared a workshop. I thank God for the chance to just chill together all day!! For the chance to laugh together, cry together, remember together. His Facebook status was so special and means so much to me—all the replies too—just made me cry. God has truly blessed me with amazing people in my life from all over the world. And Dave's networking has been so special to keep all those people in the loop.[1]

Despite the wonderful relationships BJ developed with people, she agonised over not being able to find someone to share life's journey as a wife and mother. There were times of intense loneliness. I remember in a number of phone calls with BJ while she was in Thailand hearing her express her loneliness. "Dad, it would just be nice to take this journey with someone at my side—so we could be a team—soul mates—someone who would understand me and love me and I could love in the same way." My heart was heavy for her. I also realised that there would be very few guys who would be able to keep up with her—who could share the same passion for Christ, for people, and for "living on the edge" so often. I prayed that whoever she found would not stunt her growth as a Christian and as a missionary. Yet, despite the personal pressures, her identity in Christ held steady.

BJ's years in the local church context at Birrong Church of the Nazarene were pivotal in her development of her concept of serving. Like parenting, pastoring a church is mostly walking day by day in obedience to the Lord, and trusting that he knows what he is doing. I am humbled to see the way God led our congregation, despite my bumbling efforts. It wasn't easy and there were days that it would have been easier to walk away from what, I felt at the time, were a fractious and self-centred people. However, God was gracious and taught me to work with his agenda, not mine. I grew to love the people who served God with a passion that was inspiring. Birrong was a small church but God graciously brought growth in spirit and in numbers through the thirteen years that I was there. Initially it was the seniors group of the church that grew in numbers. We were after all situated in the community with an aging population. However, we were also in an area that had four reasonably large high schools; many young people were a part of the community as well.

This provided an interesting dynamic for the local congregation. We had a good number of seniors as well as a good number of high schoolers

---

1. BJ diary, Jan 13, 2012.

and young adults. Add to this a growing number of Pacific Islanders, and members of a few other cultures in small numbers and we had a challenging setting. I thank God for mature Christian leaders in the church who discerned God at work and let him do some extraordinary things. We began to articulate, as a local expression of our denominational values (we are Christian, holiness and missional), our own congregational values that we felt God had called us to express in all that we did.

1. We placed a value on making it as easy as possible for people to respond positively to the gospel. We did not want to put road blocks in the way of people coming to Christ using Acts 15:28 as our example. Come to Christ first and then let him work on the lifestyle and ethical issues in this new walk.

2. We placed a value on pulling down barriers—building bridges between each other using Galatians 3:26–28 as our reality. We recognised that the natural tendency with our diverse congregation would be to splinter into different homogenous groups. However we wanted to express kingdom values and affirm our diversity within our oneness in Christ. We wanted to express a mutual respect for each other in all that we did.

3. We placed a value on making disciples. When people came to Christ, we wanted them to learn to live in faith and walk as Jesus walked based on Matt 28:19–20. We wanted everyone to be in an effective small group, learning to walk as a Christian in a holistic manner.

Under the leadership of Rev. David Harris, the youth of the church began to see that their activities were not about entertaining themselves, but rather in serving. Each month the youth would make care calls on seniors in the community and serve them in some way—cleaning windows, cleaning house, taking away trash, etc. I would talk to the seniors about sharing their lives with young people and allowing the young people to serve the seniors in some small way. We established within the DNA of the church youth a service mentality. Sunday was always a time of thanking God for each other and for acts of service and random acts of kindness. Once a quarter the youth would have "Friends Night." Youth were expected to bring along a friend that had not been to youth group before. Unless the regulars brought a new friend, they could not attend that particular night! Often youth members would share "new" friends so that they could participate. This created a wonderful sense of excitement and pushed young people to invite their schoolmates to the youth night, which was always designed as a social time of fun. This way the DNA of the group developed as service and outreach.

The seniors developed a core group of lay pastors who would make contact with a large number of seniors each month to ensure that they were doing OK. Hospital visits, telephone calls, social outings for coffee all became a normal part of the routine for the seniors group—many of whom were finding Christ in a personal way for the first time in their lives. In gatherings that included young and old (for example the Sunday morning worship service) young people would look out for seniors and help them from their cars to the church building. Seniors would eagerly track down a young person they had been praying for during the week and check how the exam had gone, or whether they were able to get that assignment in on time. I was humbled to see the Christian community at work, and our regular family altar times at church were times of spontaneous testimonies to Christ's love being expressed through people caring for people. Loving God through loving people was the norm in this community of faith.

Young people came to meetings and sat on the front rows of the church, not the back. An expectancy and enthusiasm were a part of the ethos. At district church functions you could always tell when the young people from the Birrong church were present—they were sitting on the front rows of the meeting place! There were regular celebration lunches when young and old ate together, cleaned up together and acted like family. Music filled the lives of young people and many times informal jamming sessions filled Sunday afternoons at the church. In summer after evening church a good number of young people would return to our house to swim in the pool and "hang out." The church community was a fun group, and we were amazed at how little prompting it took to get our children to church.

The multigenerational interaction was a feature of the Birrong church that brought a maturity and growth in discipleship right across the church community. Harkness says:

> Acceptance and affirmation is enhanced by intergenerational contact. Optimal faith development cannot happen in social isolation, for persons' sense of acceptance by God and their own self-identity is closely related to their acceptance by and of other people. . . . Faith development is linked closely to the quality of relationships one has, especially with people for whom the key commonality is seeking "to do God's will." . . . Thus "a congregation does a

disservice when it completely delegates nurture [of its members] to specialised age-level ministries."

Adulthood, however, is often perceived as a fairly static, monolithic stage marked by a sense of "having arrived"—and many adults seem to have stayed with a faith and view of God that stopped developing at about the same time they left behind their "spiritual growing and learning days" (e.g. upon leaving Sunday School). The irony in this is that they have stayed with a childish faith but left behind the childlike qualities expected of the disciple of Jesus Christ. Interacting with people from other generational groups can help to redress this state of affairs.[2]

These experiences were fundamental in shaping BJ's ministry perspective. The influence of the Birrong youth group ministry formation along with the intergenerational context cannot be overestimated.

In a sermon, BJ speaks of the influence of Pastor David in her life and the Birrong church experience:

> I am so grateful for a mentor who walked with me! He discipled me . . . in the harvest . . . as we worked together . . . I was being prepared . . . I was being equipped. From my early youth days my mentor used me in the leadership of our youth group, actually developing a youth group. He taught me how to lead and how to run activities . . . until I could then do it myself. He took time out for me . . . took interest in what was going on in my life. We met regularly to catch up, something that continues to this day whenever we are in the same town! . . . or through skype etc. He let me make mistakes and guided me through picking up pieces. He stood by me, he supported me. He saw the areas of leadership to develop in me and in time had me running my own discipleship groups; something which I have been able to develop everywhere I go. I would not be where I am today if it were not for my mentor, my discipler, my friend.[3]

As BJ developed her ministry skills and deepened her personal walk with the Lord, she let her light shine at high school. A Christian teacher at the school noticed BJ and asked whether she would assist in starting an "Interschool Christian Fellowship" (ISCF). This is a gathering of Christian students who meet over lunchtime about once a week for prayer, Bible

---

2. Allan Harkness, "Intergenerationality: Biblical and Theological Foundations," *Christian Education Journal*, ser. 3, 9 (2012) 130.

3. Belinda Allder, unpublished sermon based on Matt 9:35–38.

study and mutual encouragement. They also plan events to reach other students with the gospel. BJ was instrumental in making the small group a "cool" place for the students to be seen. These Christian young people courageously became a positive influence in a very secular, multicultural school. At a time when racial tension occasionally flared into violence between groups in the school ground, a positive, inclusive group of students praying for their school was both needed and refreshing. It is interesting to observe that BJ didn't just make friends with fellow Christians. She had a wide circle of non-Christian friends with whom she kept contact through e-mail, Facebook, etc. Several travelled to see her while she was battling cancer and she was an amazing witness to Christ's grace to these friends.

The key experience that BJ referred to as her missionary calling came in a rather dramatic fashion. As a further expression of youth called to serve and reach out, Youth in Mission teams were developed from the local congregation. These were designed to move young people out of their comfort zone, move into areas where they would need to intentionally cross cultural barriers, and ultimately rely on God to lead and empower them in unique ways. One such Youth in Mission trip was to Fiji. Little did I realise just how much out of their comfort zone they would be on that first trip to Fiji!

Pastor David Harris outlined a process of application and preparation to the young people of the church and, ultimately, five young people, chaperoned by David himself, were selected for the trip.[4] For six months prior to the trip each team member was given a daily devotional guide to follow and then each week the team would meet to share their spiritual journey, develop skills for the tasks required on the trip, and begin to use their gifts in the local church setting. The expectations placed upon the team were high. These were not externally driven expectations, but rather jointly arrived at after they discussed what they thought ought to be expected of such a team. They thought through what might be useful for uniting the team so that they operated as a team. The resultant team standard was probably higher than one might impose from outside the group. It was a group of highly committed, enthusiastic, well-prepared young people who were ready to tackle whatever the mission trip experience threw at them. There was no doubt that this team became the "cream of the crop" of the youth group, not through any natural abilities they may have had, but through hard work, and a willingness to be sold out to Jesus.

---

4. The young people chosen were: BJ, Caine Pennell, Andrew Myles, Kylie Harris, and Adam Boyd (from another Nazarene church in Sydney).

Most of the trip was predictable as far as youth in mission trips go. Perhaps the greatest strength of the team was its flexibility in changing circumstances and their willingness to cheerfully "go with the flow." The field strategy coordinator for the South Pacific at the time, Rev. James Johnson, spoke of the strength of the team. When given a choice, he said, he would always choose a team such as this one, over other possibilities because of their sensitivity to culture and their ability to get in and do the job, whatever that would require. This reputation, I think, was the result of excellent preparation and also seeing modelled a dynamic Christian community at the Birrong church where ministry skills were regularly exercised.

The team was seen very much as an extension of the Birrong church. Regular prayer times for each member of the team were held; seniors assisted in raising money for the expenses of the team; and when it came time to go, the church community gathered for an inspiring and challenging sending service. They were sent with our blessing, sent in the name of Jesus, and sent knowing that every day they were being supported in prayer by their sending community. Other young people formed part of the support base by keeping communication flowing from the team to the church.

Toward the end of the trip, the Fiji Nazarene church heard that it was possible for our team to go to the Yasawa Islands, a group of remote islands that the Nazarene church had been seeking to reach. A church plant was their goal. Pastor David organised a boat to ferry the team to the islands, supposedly about a three-hour journey across the open sea. Once again, hindsight is a wonderful thing, but I am glad that I did not know of the details of the trip until the team returned. It seemed that the trip to these islands was plagued with trouble right from the start. There was an extensive delay in getting the boat, and so it wasn't until early afternoon that the owner of the boat was ready to leave. This boat was no luxurious cruiser. It was little more than a dinghy with one small outboard motor; it was loaded with goods for people in these remote islands, and our team jumped on board in good faith. BJ told of the long journey, the smell of the petrol fumes, cramped conditions, and the lack of shade from the hot sun. While the sea was not rough, the waves had the little boat bobbing up and down like a cork. All the team members were seasick. This was not turning out to be a fun trip at all!

After several hours of not seeing land at all, the team began to worry about getting to their destination. They were sick, covered in salt spray, wet, and wanting this experience to be over! The time for their arrival passed, and they still appeared far from land. Darkness began to fall, and Pastor David's frequent questions to the skipper of the boat about their arrival time were met with the usual vague, nonchalant response. As the sun set and stars began to fill a beautiful South Pacific sky, Pastor David became more insistent. As far as he was concerned, they were lost at sea! His normal brown Tongan face was white with concern, and his happy disposition had left him the last time he had to lean over the side of the boat and empty what little remained of the contents of his stomach. "Find the nearest piece of land and let's spend the night on the beach! We can go on to the islands in the daylight tomorrow!" This was his request that became an insistent plea and then a demand.

Eventually, the skipper of the boat complied and he managed to find a beach for the night. The team, grateful for some solid ground, quickly made themselves comfortable for the night! Wow! Talk about resiliency and being pushed out of their comfort zone! However, it was while the boat was still at sea that BJ was lying looking up at the amazing sky, feeling sick and worrying over the fact that they were lost at sea. Thoughts of never seeing her family again, drowning in an ocean where no one would ever find them, wondering why they ever decided to come on this trip filled her trembling heart. Then in a spiritual moment, as she looked up into a sky she had never seen as beautiful before, she felt the Lord say to her, "I am the Lord of this sky. This is the same sky that your parents are under. People are the same everywhere under this sky. Many feel as lost as you feel right now. I want you to serve me under this sky." BJ's response was one of, "Of course! You have my life in Your hands. I am Yours!" From that moment a peace came upon her and her signature was born. BJ would serve her Lord and Saviour *under his sky!* Every time BJ signed off an e-mail, letter, or a report, she did so with the words, "Under His Sky—BJ." This was a reminder to herself that she had received a call to serve, and an acknowledgment that she would do so under the Lordship of Jesus Christ in his world.

The night sky and stars continued to have a special place in BJ's heart. Many times she felt closer to God as she gazed heavenward. Gayle Boss writes:

> So the Spirit prompts Jesus after his baptism. After the exhilaration of "this is my beloved Son, with whom I am well pleased" (Matt. 3:17, RSV), Jesus is going to face the "Oh, really?" of the Adversary. The sorrow rooted in doubt is on its way to meet him. So the Spirit sends him, alone, to a wild place. We typically think

of this desert depleting Jesus. Though it didn't supply him much actual food and water, the raw beauty of the place fed and trained his soul to resist the temptations ahead. Away from disciples and detractors, family members, the synagogue, the carpenter shop, and the marketplace, absorbed in the severe majesty of the desert, Jesus can sense most forcefully the presence and power of God. Spoken into the air of that presence, the taunting of Satan are tinny and thin.

Job was a slower study than Jesus. After he and his friends spend 889 verses wrangling over the reason for his suffering and God's part in it, God finally steps in and says, in effect, what Mary Oliver says: "Come outside and pay attention." No explanation of the divine logic of suffering, just look.

When Job has taken in with rapt attention wonders like the ocean and the lion and leviathan, he confesses, "I had heard of thee by the hearing of the ear, but now my eye sees thee" (Job 42:5, RSV). His sorrow has been subdued, and not through the weaponry of reason, but through pure abandonment—allowing himself to be attentively submerged in a wondrous creation. He then finds . . . that he can't even remember the questions that so burdened him.[5]

The Apostle Paul's declaration comes to mind:

> Ever since the creation of the world his (God's) eternal power and divine nature, invisible though they are, have been understood and seen through the things he has made. (Rom 1:20 NRSV)

The story of the trip does not end with safe haven on the beach! The next morning, the skipper loaded the team on board, and with another three hours on the sea, they finally arrived at the Yasawa Islands. Gratefully the team stepped once again onto dry land and gathered their possessions ready to hike to the village. Before starting out, Pastor David was met by a representative from the village. Protocol required that David, as team leader, ask permission of the chief to reside in the village for few days. Pastor David was also required to explain the kinds of things that the team would like to do in the village. The team had in mind typical youth in mission activities working with children, meeting with adults and inviting people to a Bible study.

However, the chief of the village was not happy at the team's arrival and refused to see Pastor David. Thankfully, Pastor David was in tune enough with the culture to realise that forcing the issue, or ignoring protocol was

---

5. Gayle Boss, "Natural Medicine," *Weavings* 27 (2012) 7.

not appropriate. Through intermediaries, Pastor David was able to find out that the chief was unhappy because, just a few days previously, a Christian group had visited the village and not followed protocol. The chief was insulted and refused to have another Christian group visit as a reaction to the offense. There was nothing that our team could do—except pray! Pastor David was able to negotiate through intermediaries to have a place to stay, and he promised the leaders that the team would not do anything unless given permission to do so.

The next couple of days the team spent relaxing on the beach and doing nothing except praying that God would open doors for them. The boat was due back to pick up the team on the third day. It appeared that this was a wasted trip! On the final afternoon the chief gave permission for the team to do some activity in the village that evening. There was much rejoicing in the team, now bored from doing nothing for two days. They anticipated having a few children to talk to in the late afternoon and early evening, so they prepared to share the gospel story through the use of the "Jesus beads."[6] Armed with plenty of "Jesus beads" they set off for the village. As they arrived, they were met by some children, and some of their parents. Within minutes of their arrival almost the entire village had gathered to hear about the "Jesus beads." Improvising, the team divided the large group into smaller groups and shared the gospel in those small groups while making the bracelets. The story was repeated time and again late into the evening. God had opened the door and what was initially thought to be a wasted effort was really the opportunity to show deep respect for the Fijian people of the Yasawa Islands. This could not have been rushed. It was time to abide by Fijian time, not Aussie time. Team members look back on this as arguably the most effective event of the whole Fiji mission experience!

I thank God for a team (and its leader!) who were patient enough to affirm other people's customs and recognise that the mission was not about what the team had planned, but how to connect effectively in grace-filled ways. Here was mission being accomplished incarnationally. You can imagine the sense of rejoicing that captured the congregation at home as they heard the team recount the adventures of their mission trip! We all thanked God for his protection and for his higher purposes that were lived out through the lives of these young people. However, you can also be

---

6. This is a simple evangelistic tool where coloured beads are strung together to make a bracelet. The colours represent some part of the gospel message and the hope is that as the person wears the newly created bracelet, they will be reminded of the gospel story.

assured that I had some specific debrief moments with Pastor David about what we expose our teams to on such trips. He was even more concerned than I about the potential for disaster, and he was glad for the chance to set some procedures in place for the protection of future teams. I still wonder, though, had Pastor David and the team not stepped out on this trip, whether the impact of the team would have been anything like it turned out to be. One of the lessons I learned in all of this was not to let the "what if" question so plague me that I am paralysed from doing what God may well be directing.

Some years later BJ shared a devotional thought with the church entitled "Out of Your Comfort Zone—Out of the Boat," based on Matthew 14:22–33.

> When we talk about short term Missions you will often hear the phrase "out of your comfort zone" . . . no matter how many times you hear this phrase, it is difficult to fully prepare yourself for that time when you have to "get out of the boat."
>
> When we are giving our lives in service to Christ we are often faced with things which we consider out of our comfort zone. When we are asked to get out of the boat, like Peter was, how do we respond? Jesus called Peter to a task He knew he could do. Yet, Peter doubted. You will find Jesus calling you to do things, in service to Him, that perhaps you didn't think you could ever do. But be assured that He is in control and He would not call you to something you cannot do.
>
> To stay "on the water" we need to keep our faith firmly in Jesus and our eyes fixed on Him. It is as we look around, as we see what the other people around us are doing, as we listen to those critics and discouragers around us, as we look at the fall before us that we begin to slip and eventually find ourselves "in the water." The devil is very clever in his attacks on us during these times. All he needs to do is hand us a pair of binoculars and make the whole thing seem even more "scary"!!
>
> I remember one time when I was out of my comfort zone. I didn't have to get out of the boat because we were lost at sea in a boat!!!! It could have been the scariest experience of my life . . . *but* . . . I remember the sign that God gave me to remind me He was in control . . . the *amazing starry night*!!! It just quickly reminded me He was in control and I had to keep my gaze fixed on Him!

BJ was soon back into active service in church life at Birrong but she had a restlessness to be doing more. Having completed three years of university and graduating with a bachelor of teaching, she decided to take a part-time teaching job and complete her bachelor of education, a further twelve months' full-time study. She found a job at a small, private Christian school at Greenacre, a suburb of Sydney that had a very multicultural population. She was only teaching part-time for a couple of months before the school offered her a full-time position teaching grade 2. She spent time talking with Jacque about this—BJ hated making decisions! Should she cut back on her studies, should she not take the job? Could she cope with doing all this? These were just some of the many questions with which she had to wrestle. Ever wise Mum suggested that she try doing both for a semester and then decide at the end of the semester how much she needed to cut back. She really only had about two months to survive being a full-time teacher and full-time student before she needed to make a further decision.

This subsequently became the path she chose. BJ successfully completed the two months and felt that she could survive another semester at that frantic pace, so continued to complete her bachelor of education in the twelve months. This experience taught her to juggle a multitude of tasks successfully. Those that knew BJ in her missionary days knew that she never sat still. There were always a multitude of things to be done, people to see, letters to write, texts to send . . . I think that her time as full-time teacher, full-time student and youth group leader in a very active youth programme at church gave her skills she would use later in her ministry. She was amazingly busy—and loving it!

The next step in this missionary call that remained so vivid to BJ was one she did not take alone. Her best friend, Mel, did her bachelor of education over a two-year period as she taught school full-time. Mel graduated a year later than BJ, but then they hatched a plan together. Both single, it was time for them to do some teaching cross-culturally and experience life outside of Australia. Both were captured by the challenge of cross-cultural teaching and decided that a year in London would be a wonderful experience. Deep down I think BJ was using this time to test the waters further regarding her call. Could she survive away from home? Did she have the skill and flexibility necessary to be effective cross culturally? Could she make her own way? BJ was always sensitive to the fact that she was a pastor's kid and never wanted the church connections to open doors for her based on her relationship with me. When introducing herself in church circles she rarely used her last name so that she didn't get the usual response, "Oh are you Bruce and Jacque's daughter?" How she hated that!! It wasn't too long into her outstanding missionary service, though, that the tables were turned and I was known as "the father of BJ." OK! I can live with that!

The time of teaching in London was life transforming. BJ saw that not only could she survive the rigors of cross-cultural work, she thrived! She and Mel lived in Watford and became active participants in the Woodside Church of the Nazarene, Watford. Within weeks they felt like it was home. Melinda reflected on this time away:

> I want to share about that year because it is probably the year I learnt the most about living authentically for and with Christ. And I learnt it all through the example of my best mate and travel buddy. I was lucky enough to spend a whole year "doing life" together with her and being coached in the same skill. I was reasonably young in my faith when we decided to go on the big adventure, which has become a bit of a rite of passage for young Australians. We would pack up all we had, move to London for a year and get some teaching work, while also using the chance to travel. It's not exactly a ground breaking idea, many had gone before us and many have followed. But it was ground breaking for us! Neither of us had lived away from Australia on our own before and we were also newly graduated teachers, still finding our feet in our new careers. How would we go being in a foreign land for so long on our own teaching in a completely different culture and system? The answer: just fine!
>
> My lessons in "doing life" began almost as soon as we'd left home shores. Our good friend Derene Els had given us each a travel devotional journal and we made a commitment right at the start to do a devotion and pray together every day. Under BJ's leadership, we honoured that commitment every single day that we were away. I'd never been so disciplined and I was loving it!
>
> We had our first stop over in Bali for 2 nights. Neither of us had been to Bali before, but we understood it to have a bit of a reputation for being a "party" destination and we arrived cautiously. One of the 2 days that we were there happened to be a Sunday, so as soon as we started nutting out an agenda, BJ suggested we try to find a church to attend Sunday morning. I'm ashamed to say the thought had not even crossed my mind, but it was no-brainer to BJ. "Of course we would try and go to church, it's Sunday!" So it was decided. BJ and I were not interested in the party scene, so we spent most of our time at the beach, or the shops, or in "Dunkin' Donuts" or playing "Uno," or eating "McFlurrys." Doesn't sound very exciting or adventurous, but we were happy!

Early into our stay we met another Aussie—a 40-year-old divorcee by the name of Wazza. He was a nice, funny guy who seemed a bit lost. He'd come away on a break to try and escape the messiness of his divorce back home. He seemed to be in need of friendship, in need of more than the shallow party atmosphere that was being offered, and he seemed to connect with us. So we hung out a bit and BJ was very deliberate in making suggestions for times of "hanging" together. He played "Uno" with us, ate "McFlurrys" with us and we helped him shop for some shirts. Then BJ suggested we ask him if he wanted to come to church with us. I couldn't believe she was suggesting it! Surely he wouldn't do that! When she put the suggestion to Wazza, he laughed and said, "Yeah, when I get home my mates will all ask me what I got up to in Bali, and I'll say, "played some 'Uno,' ate some 'McFlurrys' and went to church! Hahahaha!!!" And then he agreed to come. I was blown away!

Unfortunately we never made it to church because we couldn't find it! No-one could really give us any helpful information or directions. So the 3 of us went to "Dunkin Donuts" instead. It was the last day in Bali and the last time we would see Wazza. Over coffee and donuts Wazza said something that I will always remember and that will warm my heart for the rest of my life. He said, "You girls are different. It's in your smiles. You're not like the other girls here who have come looking for something. You've already found what you are looking for." It was the first time someone had seen Jesus in me and expressed it. And it was all because we "walked slowly" with someone in need, and we were just being ourselves. We invited Wazza in to do life with us for 2 days and God used us! My Christian walk was impacted that day in a way that will last into eternity. It was my first lesson in "doing life." You can only imagine how the rest of the year played out!

Upon reflection, it is so obvious that God created BJ to be a missionary. It really came as no surprise when she told me of her calling. I was relieved when she told me as I just knew she would not be truly satisfied or truly fulfilled in any other role. I am thankful beyond measure that for her last two and a half years we lived only a couple of hundred metres apart from each other. We spent that time "doing life" together and I continued to learn from my soul mate, from the way she handled her cancer journey with hope, grace, dignity, and steadfast faith.[7]

---

7. Melinda Good, e-mail message to author, Sept 15, 2013.

The Calling

During the summer of 2001, it was time for a break from teaching, so they decided to journey to the United States to attend the general assembly of the Church of the Nazarene. It became a time of getting reacquainted with members of US Youth in Mission team members who had visited Australia at some point. After the general assembly they then travelled most of the United States via Greyhound bus. Now I am sure that the Greyhound bus company is a wonderful company, but BJ and Mel had some truly hair-raising experiences! One time a bus caught on fire and there had to be an emergency evacuation. Another time an armed passenger decided to wave his firearm around in a generally threatening way. Police were called to resolve the situation. It also seemed to BJ that most of the bus stations were in the seedy parts of town and so layovers late at night were always a challenge. What an experience!

It was while BJ was in England that she began recognising a call to missions in a tangible way. For those of us observing BJ, we could see that this was almost a given. Her predisposition to mix cross-culturally, her obvious abilities to communicate well, and her love of people and life all pointed to a special kind of calling. This was not so obvious to BJ. She agonised over this call, and eventually wrote a letter to me saying,

> I don't know how to say this, Dad, and it scares me half to death, but I think God is calling me to mission work! This is frightening and I don't know what to do about this, except to say "Yes."

The letter continued to express her fear of the unknown, the uncertainty about where she might serve, and the pain of leaving friends behind. Self-doubt was clearly evident in the letter. Being a pastor's kid she had grown up observing, and many times living through, the stresses and strains of ministry. There were times when the church lacked understanding and we felt used and abused as a family. But we also experienced times of absolute exhilaration at seeing God work in remarkable ways. BJ had seen both the agony and ecstasy of ministry, and she was uncertain whether she had the strength to weather it all. My response to her was, "Just say, 'Yes!' And let the Lord work out the details."

I must admit that there was a part of me as a father, and Jacque as a mother, that struggled with releasing BJ to this calling. While we didn't know the specifics of what she would face, we knew that she would be stretched and would struggle with some of the demands of such a ministry. We wanted to protect her from those difficult times; after all, she was our baby girl! However, we also knew that there was no better place to be than in the centre of God's will, doing what God had called her to be and do. It was not surprising that one of her favourite songs became "Yes, Lord, Yes," by Shirley Caesar.

BJ's positive response to the "scary" call to missions led her to contact the Asia Pacific Regional Office for the Church of the Nazarene. Her request was simply, "Do you have a place where I can serve?" After going through the usual form filling, contract reviews, etc., BJ was asked to consider twelve months' voluntary service in either East Timor or Thailand. The first twelve months was another experiment in following God into the unknown. She had already proved to herself that she could work outside of Australia. She had proved that she could survive financially and also be energised by the challenges. It was time to take the next step.

> Now the Lord said to Abram, "Go from your country and your kindred and your father's house to the land that I will show you."
> (Gen 12:1 NRSV)

Chapter 3

The Missionary

BJ's formal missionary journey really began as a volunteer English teacher at the Maetang Tribal Children's Home in northern Thailand. Initially she was open to a placement anywhere on the Asia Pacific Region by the Church of the Nazarene. Two places were suggested: East Timor and Thailand. She chose Thailand, not because of any particular love for Thailand over East Timor at the time, but because she thought the assignment had more of a teaching focus. Additionally, there was another young lady in Australia who was considering going to East Timor to assist. BJ did not want to overlap with her ministry, although they had been good friends for a number of years. The other young lady did ultimately volunteer for a few months in East Timor.

BJ took various leadership and personality assessment profiles so that she could not only understand herself, but also be placed appropriately by mission leadership. Her signature themes for the Clifton StrengthsFinder[1] assessment were: Developer, Individualization, Arranger, Harmony, and Belief. She further developed her self-understanding by using the Style of Influence[2] assessment tool and was described as a "supportive specialist" in SOI terms. It is these styles and gifting that BJ brought to the missionary task in Thailand.

Her time in Thailand began in July 2002 with three months of language study in Bangkok. She stayed with missionary Lisa Lehman in her apartment and loved the feel of the big city. Given her preference she would have stayed in big cities that reminded her of home (Sydney). She loved the pace, the variety, and the multicultural feel of large cities. It may sound glib, but BJ really did have the gift for learning languages. Thai is so different from English, not only in alphabet, but also in tone and expression. Her

---

1. "Lead with Your Strengths," Gallup Strengths Center, http://www.gallupstrengthscenter.com/home.

2. Style of Influence, http://www.thesoi.com/index.php?s-of-influence.

confidence and enthusiasm for connecting with people had her immersing herself in Thai speaking contexts. She learned quickly. In a few short weeks she was able to hold simple conversations in Thai and it seemed that her winsome personality had people eager to engage in those conversations with her.

Lisa Lehman recalls:

> Belinda arrived in Bangkok to begin Thai language study just a little over a year after I had come to the field. So we learned and explored a lot of Thai life, language and ministry together from the beginning. Almost from the start, though, I was her "Pi" (big sister). I looked up to her in many ways for her personal bridge-building skills with people. She looked up to me for Thai language skill, but in many ways I learned from her example even in Thai language learning too.

Family visited BJ some six months after she had arrived in Thailand, and she was our confident tour guide. Taxi drivers, hotel staff, and tour operators all commented on her ability to speak Thai. We were amazed. To us, as parents, it was a confirmation that BJ was in the right place. In 2007, several years after those first tentative steps into the Thai language, BJ wrote in one of her update letters:

> I am thankful for the opportunity to live and serve in Thailand. This week I had a funny experience . . . instead of the usual "your Thai is so good" comments when meeting someone for the first time, I got "you look a lot like a foreigner" (instead of the wow, a foreigner speaking Thai). It was more like a Thai that looks like a foreigner! Crazy![3]

This is high praise indeed for her proficiency in language and an achievement that she celebrated. She wanted to be considered so much a part of the Thai context that her "foreignness" was no longer a barrier. BJ wrote for her evangelism class:

> Our witness allows people to experience and access God through our story. . . .
>
> Incarnational Evangelism is *being* Jesus in the world, and thus proclaiming the gospel message. The message will therefore come in many forms as the messenger is used in a variety of situations.
>
> "To act incarnationally therefore will mean, in part, that in our mission to those outside of the faith, we will need to exercise

---

3. Belinda Allder, update newsletter, Dec 2007.

a genuine identification and affinity with those we are attempting to reach."[4] Relational evangelism places a high value on people. It involves entering people's worlds, in all aspects. Incarnational Evangelism takes relationships a step further, insuring that it is not just "us" but God himself that is entering into their worlds.

Relational evangelism has been described as similar to a railway track. It has 2 tracks, one representing the content (the Gospel) and the other the incarnation (our lives). However, one might argue that to be truly incarnational the content and our "lives" should be one and the same, therefore it may be better illustrated as a monorail (singular) track. . . .

If we compartmentalize our evangelism . . . we make "evangelism" an event, an event that requires a given result. It is based on numbers, results and responses. Incarnational evangelism is based more on quality than quantity. It is a shift away from cognitive programs and a move towards relational processes. . . .

As Christians that are "with" God, filled with the Holy Spirit, we can't help but participate in this act called evangelism. It is not an act we go out to intentionally do, but rather an act that happens as a consequence of our relationship with Christ. . . .

Traditional ways of invitation and response are demonstrated in Jesus' life, but they are grounded in relationship. Jesus invites and allows opportunity to respond to him by reciprocating his embrace of them. He also welcomes people into community. Jesus also shows us to embrace people where they are, before they are cleaned, before they are healed, before they have accepted him. Jesus invites people to "follow me." He invites people into the journey. The invitation is not individually based, but rather an invitation into the community. The invitation to a journey illustrates that the "message" is alive and continuing. The "message" we are communicating (as was Jesus) does not end with salvation. The "message" takes us into discipleship and the continuing encounters with God.

Living incarnationally, our lives, and thus our witness, will include "presence," "proximity," "powerlessness," and "proclamation." As one lives in the community, and becomes part of the very fabric of the community, "presence" is met. It is not enough to merely "think" as they do, or to place ourselves in communities for short periods of time, but rather a long term commitment with no time limits or expectations placed on it. The "message" we present must be an indigenous one and not a "western" or "our

---

4. Alan Hirsch, *The Forgotten Ways: Reactivating the Missional Church* (Grand Rapids: Brazos, 2007), 133.

churched culture" transplant. "Proximity" occurs as we move into their communities, and not just as a "presence" but available and involved in this long-term commitment. "Powerlessness" is demonstrating love through humility. . . .

There still needs to be a place for the proclamation of the Word. Often in relational evangelism, it is all about the relationship and the real message of who Jesus Christ is can get lost. It is in this "grey" area that we too often turn to programs and textbook answers. The changing method of communication also can lead to this loss of message. This need not necessarily be the case, however. In the same way that Jesus did not deny his divinity in assuming human form, neither need the church deny its eternal ontological holiness in becoming culturally relevant.

"The church that has undertaken that kind of incarnational ministry . . . has placed itself on the line with the poor and is a church that gains a profound respect from that community. In being willing to lose its life, it saves it. The people of the community will listen to that church, will listen to what it has to say and the gospel it has to proclaim."[5]

There are some key principles or dangers that keep us from engaging in incarnational evangelism. The use of jargon that create barriers can be a major hindrance. We (the Christian community) use terminology and see things as "insiders" and "outsiders." The terminology excludes people on "understanding" grounds. A "message" which may make sense to us, may have no meaning to the listener. In being incarnational we are able to contextualize our message. The use of "us" and "them" words also make the idea of "conversion" a black and white concept, and thus also alludes to a precise moment of decision. "Conversion is depicted (in the Old Testament) not as a singular event but as an ongoing process of realignment with God." We base our gospel message on "head" knowledge, rather than encountering a relationship with Jesus Christ. We try and be relational in our initial encounters but then move into a "head" knowledge presentation of the gospel.

Another area keeping us from true incarnational evangelism is "fake" relationships. Our relationships can be shallow, and still based on evangelism as a means to an end. We seek to build relationships in order to present the gospel, and "convert" a life, rather than making relationships out of a real love for the other person. The "symbol" or "sign" that should be demonstrated through our lives is not genuine. "The reason why anyone refuses to assent to your opinion, or his aid to your benevolent design, is in you. He

---

5. Robert Linthicum, *Empowering the Poor* (Monrovia, CA: MARC, 1991), 113.

refuses to accept you as a bringer of truth, because, though you think you have it, he feels that you have it not. You have not given him the authentic sign."[6] . . .

Too often for us, incarnation is an ideal we aspire to without becoming a lifestyle we embrace. To fully redeem this notion for ministry, we must redeem the costly nature of the act itself. Once this has been redeemed, we are in a better position to reflect on the costly nature of Christian ministry itself.

This paper reflects the passions of BJ: her intense desire to live authentically; the developing of relationships with a wide variety of people; her high value and respect for people; her disciplined approach to her own spiritual walk. Many times while home with us, she would have friends stay with her for a few days. Each day, there would be a time of reading the Word and praying devotionally with whoever was visiting. It wasn't a long time spent doing this, but it was done each day, and it was an important part of her schedule. The discipline was not a rigid habit, because the time she would turn to the Scripture would vary upon what she was doing in that day. Her favourite devotional reading book was *Every Day with Jesus*, by Selwyn Hughes. These daily readings were purchased in booklet form by her grandmother. It was "Grandma Dudley's" way of being a part of BJ's journey. It also happens to be Grandma Dudley's favourite daily devotional guide as well.

BJ became a student of culture (particularly the Thai and Hill Tribe cultures) and in another paper she gave a brief description of the context of her ministry setting—the Maetang Tribal Children's Home.

> Maetang Tribal Children's Home was founded in 1984 by 3 men who saw a need for educating their people. These 3 men were Samuel Yangmi, Lubae Jasa and Silas Jasa. All 3 of these men are related (blood and marriage) and are a part of a large Lahu (*one of the Hill Tribes of northern Thailand*) family. They saw the need to have access to schools for people who live in villages. In those days there were usually no schools in the village and therefore most village children were not getting an education. A dormitory was set up in Maetang to meet this need. The land was bought at a location that was close to a good primary and high school, so that the students could walk to their schools. Maetang is a farming community in Chiang Mai province, 45km from Chiang Mai city. The

---

6. George Hunter, *The Celtic Way of Evangelism: How Evangelism Can Reach the West Again* (Grand Rapids: Abingdon 2000), 57.

Home also sought to give these children a Christian environment to grow up in and teach them Christianity, which is different from the Buddhist teachings they would receive at school.

The home was established with a handful of children and the Lubae family acting as dorm parents. It was first established to run like an extended family. In 1993, Samuel Yangmi joined the Church of the Nazarene and all of his ministries joined too. Thus, began the relationship between the Church of the Nazarene and Maetang Tribal Children's Home.

Assisted with contribution from sponsors through Nazarene Compassionate Ministries, and with some support coming from their parents, many of these tribal youth are now graduating from high school and becoming educated leaders of our growing tribal churches in Thailand. In addition, these youth become the open doors to establishing churches in new tribal villages. It is a great combination of compassion, education and evangelism at work in the Church.

Nazarene Compassionate Ministries, specifically the Child Sponsorship program, oversees this program for the Church of the Nazarene.

All children at the Children's Home are sponsored and must meet requirements for this program. The children at this home are not orphans. They come under the "educate a child" program. All funds that are sent through this program go to the running of the Children's Home. The funds come through to the home monthly. The children are then required to write to their sponsors a minimum of 4 times a year.

Nazarene Compassionate Ministries' Child Development program recognizes the importance of children and believes that a child's development is a process of realizing the full potential of human life as God intended it to be. NCM Child Development helps children understand that God loves them, that they are created in God's image, that they are valued and have dignity, and that they can have a personal relationship with Jesus Christ. Through our holistic approach to child development, children have the opportunity to receive food, education, life skills, and spiritual guidance.

My role began in 2002. Time itself has led to an increased responsibility in this place. The longer you are here the more respect and responsibility you get. Living on site at the Children's Home brings a lot of unofficial leadership opportunities.

I do have some official roles. I am now overseeing the sponsorship program. In this role I must make sure all information is kept up to date and entered in the global data base. I must also make sure that each child writes to their sponsor and the letters are translated. I do not work with the funding involved in this program.

I also manage our volunteer program at the Children's Home. This is an international program. We have volunteers come to help out for a couple of days up to several years. My role is to make this possible for them and make sure all of their needs associated with volunteering are met (e.g. Language study, timetables in schools, visas).

I teach English in the local schools and run an English program for the children of the Home in the evenings. Outside of the Home, I also oversee the Youth department of our church for South East Asia, including youth development. This includes overseeing any youth mission teams that may come to work in South East Asia.

Thai culture is very enriched in a "high power distance" and this is generally accepted by all. "Large power distance cultures are characterised by the acceptance of human inequality and individuals show deep respect for authority that results in a paternalistic work relationship between superior and subordinate."[7]

In all levels of society there is a Phu Yai (bigger person) / Phu Noi (smaller person) custom. It is important for a Thai person to establish an understanding of their place in a relationship very quickly, so they may ask personal questions upon meeting someone for the first time (e.g. Where do you work? How much do you earn?). Once this is established one would know the behaviour, actions and obligations expected of them. A set of mutual obligations requires Phu Noi to defer to Phu Yai through demonstrations of obedience and respect. In return Phu Yai are obligated to care for and offer assistance to Phu Noi they have regular contact with. Phu Noi may ask Phu Yai for favours such as financial help or assistance securing employment. It would cause Phu Yai some loss of face to refuse these favours. When eating out in restaurants, Phu Yai will normally settle the bill.

Thai organisations hold a vertical structure system where the flow is always upward. The ultimate superior holds much power and makes the decisions. It is a paternalistic, authoritative style of leadership that is often based on social position, wealth or family. However, it is not all . . . counter relational. This idea of it being in contradiction may just come out of our western thinking and views of leadership. "In the West, power is associated with domination,

---

7. Therese A. Joiner et al., "Traditional Leadership in Thailand: The Role of Applying Abilities for Mutual Benefit," *Journal of International Business and Economics* 9 (2009) 86.

coercion and authoritarianism; Asian cultures view power as the responsibility to nurture and support the less powerful."[8] These statements about the "West" are particularly true of Australia. In Australia power can have such negative connotations and goes against what is seen as Australian "culture." "Power" and "relationship" do not go easily together in Australian society. This is seen very differently in an Asian context. Relational aspects are a part of Thai leadership. A close relationship between leader and follower, and responsibility to each other is valued in traditional, paternalistic Thai leadership.

One of the specific ways that BJ's mode of operation can be seen is in her account of leadership development that she initiated at the Maetang Tribal Children's Home. This is an application of the incarnational approach to evangelism within the Thai and Hill Tribe cultures in which she lived. Written as part of an assessment piece for a leadership class, portions of her work illustrate her method and reasons for such an approach.

> Seeing the need to build leadership among the children at the Children's Home I have established a Youth in Mission program. This program came out of the need to make a visiting team's time in Thailand effective and benefiting the local people and church. Many teams come to help out at the Children's Home from foreign countries. Two main youth / young adult teams come regularly each year. One, a larger team of 10–15 members come for 3 weeks and another of 2–5 members come for a period of 6–8 weeks. In order to develop our local children I have established teams each year (that have gone through an application process and fit into the age limits and criteria set out). These local teams then join with the "visiting" teams. It then becomes one combined team where everyone is learning together and growing together. This program uses a Transformational Leadership approach with a large emphasis on mentoring.
>
> The program is "value added" and moves from transforming individuals to transforming communities. The two main aims of this program are:
>
> - develop the child spiritually—in the faith and Christian service
> - develop the child educationally—through time with foreigners they will develop their English, and have a greater worldview.

---

8. "Geert Hofstede Cultural Dimensions," Clearly Cultural, http://www.clearlycultural.com/geert-hofstede-cultural-dimensions.

These are the key values that are to be added through this process. These are also the key values of MTCH. The children who go through this intentional, leadership development program then in turn become the student leaders of the children's home. They are well respected among the other children, and create enthusiasm in the program.

It is clear that her inclusive nature, her desire to equip and empower others for service, and the participatory and experiential nature of the learning that took place, was consistent with her own developmental strategies and experience. The model for the Youth in Mission teams that BJ developed at the home explicitly illustrate this:

Stage 1: Application

The foreign team ran their recruitment process. The Thai team: Students from Grade 9–12 could apply to be on the Youth In Mission team. The application consists of 2 parts. The first part the student must write out their testimony (how they came to know Christ, their life as a Christian). In the second part the student must answer the question—Why do you want to be on this team?

Stage 2: Selection Process

The staff/leadership of Maetang Tribal Children's Home (MTCH) looks over the application forms and selects a team. The team size can vary depending on the number of applicants, what the team will be doing, duration of team time and so on.

Stage 3: The Team Begins to Meet Together

The team meet regularly to build relationships and work together. These group meeting times should consist of prayer time together. A translator will be needed for at least the first few meetings.

Stage 4: The Team Works Together

What the team actually does together depends on the ministry they are able to be involved in. This could include: teaching community English classes, VBS, working in local churches—songs, skits, Sunday School, outreach programs.

Stage 5: Debriefing

It is really important that everyone has the chance to analyse their experience. This is essential for the individual but also for the program.

Stage 6: The Local Team Continues to Lead at MTCH

The aim of the program is to build leaders. At the end of the "team" time we must be left with leaders who will impact their community.[9]

The specific outcomes sought in this ministry strategy are included in the final step. BJ would have considered this a circular process where the new leaders would then (and in fact did) become involved in the next round of Youth in Mission trips the following year. The whole process would then re-engage the following year. It is important to note, though, that BJ was very specific about the outcomes she felt needed to be achieved. The classic mentoring model of "you watch while I do, now let's do it together, now you do and I will watch" appears to be embedded in this strategy. Her modelling of the process, her ability to establish relational connections quickly, and her drive and energy, were features of this process.

BJ's passionate engagement with people extended well beyond her connections with the children of the home. Work colleagues, Peter and Leanne Clarke, who volunteered two years at Maetang (one year with BJ and one year without her physical presence while she started her battle with cancer back in Australia) express the challenge of working with one who was so passionate about her calling:

> There are those special few that the Lord has put with us, whose impact is truly life-transforming. Our Thai mum and sister—Belinda (BJ)—you have been one of those people for us. It's not only that we really admire the way you do things. It's that, as we do things now, we see your energy in us doing them in ways that are just like you would do them. We find ourselves trying to do things and look at situations the way you do. We exhaust people in ways that we never did before. Our resolve to serve God by loving His people is stronger and has been shaped by our experience of doing it with you. It is to the point that neither of us can any longer

---

9. Belinda Allder, unpublished paper for a leadership class at NTC, 2010.

imagine ourselves being any other way than the way we are because we walked along with you in life and in ministry.[10]

BJ continued to describe her approach to this youth in mission strategy:

> It is crucial that all team members own the mission strategy. The leader must be constantly working with the team on this and bringing it to their attention in a variety of ways. Stanley, in his talk "Making Vision Stick"[11] says this can be done by "casting vision," "celebrating vision" and "living it continuously."
>
> Having approachable leadership and trusting relationships will also help the team experience. This is also crucial when dealing with this age group. They need to feel safe and also feel needed in the team. "The team must trust the leader, and they must know that the leader trusts them. And they must trust each other."[12]
>
> There are many problems that this type of program must face. One obvious one is the initial language problem. All members (both foreign and local) see this as a major problem at the start, but I see it as a part of their development as they work through how to make it work. This also becomes a substitute for leadership.[13] By the end of the time the team is very close and communicating fine (in whatever way they have discovered to work). . . . Learning is made through experience.
>
> The team members must all be a part of the process. When leadership does not allow for this there can be confusion and disunity in the team. Asian styles of education and leadership often involve not questioning and not engaging in the process. "The lack of debate and open discussion will make the leadership team vulnerable to what they don't know, or don't know to ask. This will often result in missed steps in the decision making process. These missed steps can quickly escalate, creating unexpected problems that end in dangerous outcomes."
>
> Crossing cultural barriers to having the local leadership run the program has slowed the process. If just left to themselves from the beginning you may see an authoritative approach . . . where

---

10. Peter Clarke and Leanne Clarke, BJ memorial service eulogy, Feb 24, 2012.

11. Andy Stanley, "Making Vision Stick," Willow Creek Global Leadership Summit, 2003.

12. Walter Wright, *Relational Leadership: A Biblical Model for Leadership Service* (Carlisle: Paternoster, 2000), 53.

13. Thomas Sergiovanni, "Why We Should Seek Substitutes for Leadership," *Educational Leadership*, Feb 1992, 43.

the team is told what to do each meeting, rather than exploring for themselves. These team members are still seen as children by the leadership (even though all are high schoolers and college age), and giving authority and power to children is rare. At this stage one must work through the aspects of releasing and trust, two key aspects in transformational leadership. To help overcome this problem, for the last year, I have involved one key leader in the process, and have had her walk alongside me as I guide and empower these team members. The modelling approach has been taken to show local leadership how to make such a program work.... This then leads to self-management. The leader no longer needs to tell the follower what to do, but they are passionate about the values too and driven by these common values.

Through this program, education (a key value of MTCH) is becoming life changing; the followers are being empowered and moved to accomplish more than what is usually expected of them. Their education is moving from a "rote learning" approach to a "hands-on," "engaged" learning approach. Their education is also holistic and taking into account all parts of life (spiritual, emotional, physical, and intellectual).

As this program (this word poorly describes what is happening as this process seeks to move from "program driven" to "people driven") builds a new leadership model at MTCH, it will begin to remove institutional elements that are evident in an organisation such as MTCH. Value adding does not happen in institutional settings. Time will tell how much the culture and ingrained leadership styles will open up to allow this to infiltrate all aspects of MTCH.

As these young people's lives are transformed, they are able to impact their communities and build up new leaders. As they follow the leadership development styles and strategies they have experienced they are able to shift away from hereditary styles of leadership, and paternalistic leadership. This process is not to throw out any "culture" but rather add to their culture. It is important that through all of this, culture is considered and proper respect given where needed. As these young people become the key leaders they can too become transformational leaders impacting their families, villages, communities, churches the church district and MTCH.

The ultimate goal is for transformation to occur in the individual's lives as they draw closer to Christ, and in turn transform their communities. Transformational leadership can leave a legacy that impacts generations to come.[14]

---

14. Belinda Allder, unpublished paper written for a leadership class at NTC, 2010.

The Missionary

Similarities can be seen between her approach here and that which she experienced in the local church through her teenage years. Admittedly there were many more complications because of the cultural and language barriers, but the principles appear to be similar. While there may be nothing new in this approach to mission, I am amazed at her well-executed application of the approach, and her resiliency in the midst of difficulties. Ever the practical missionary, she was impatient with theories that did not translate well into practice. This approach translated well cross-culturally. Her approach to the language "problem" is typical of the participatory, experiential and constructivist learning approach that BJ was committed to.

Nevertheless, she acknowledged that the participatory emphasis in her strategy was countercultural in key components: relationally egalitarian rather than traditional authority based, experiential learning rather than rote learning, and integrative rather than theoretical. She did, however, see the whole process as educative and thought in terms of educational outcomes and process. Forever the teacher!

BJ's work with the many volunteers who came to Thailand was also a ministry in itself. Some came for a few weeks, others for several months. Some came as individuals, some as married couples and some as whole families. Regardless of the "package," BJ was welcoming, inclusive, and appreciative of each one. She was very comfortable in working with volunteers as part of her team. Her work at the local schools became her platform of service into the community and she was able to coordinate a number of volunteers in teaching English in those schools. Most volunteers came with the expectation that they would be involved in teaching English at the schools as their primary function. Her facility with the Thai language made her a natural bridge between the school and the various English teachers. It was, in fact, the local school that sponsored her visa in Thailand. Over her office door at the school was the grand title "English and International Relations." The acceptance of the school to her ministry and their willingness to broker the visa arrangements enabled a greater freedom of movement and responsibility than might otherwise have been possible. She loved being at the school and they loved having her.

Lisa Lehman, missionary to Thailand, tells of her connection with Wilaipun, a Thai English teacher at the local high school. She describes Wilaipun as a seeker after God who asked many questions. She was very supportive of Christians coming to assist in the English program at the school, and Lisa was accepted by the English teaching staff. This laid an important foundation for BJ as she took over the English teaching. Lisa was reassigned to Bangkok by the church. Lisa writes:

> I was deeply grateful that Belinda treasured personal time spent with the teachers and students at Maetang. She was gifted in ways I lacked to communicate beyond specific vocabulary, though her Thai vocabulary increased rapidly because she just loved to talk to everyone! I was more apt to listen and respond to conversation which others initiated. Belinda would just jump in and talk about anything! And her genuine interest in others drew them in through shared common experiences.
>
> Belinda's ministry at Maetang developed more than just her own relationships and language skills. She built lasting relationships with the English teachers and even the administration of Maetang School, which opened the door wide for a host of volunteer English teachers to be shared between the Church of the Nazarene (via Maetang Tribal Children's Home) and Maetang School.
>
> Wilaipun remained a key proponent in those relationships as well until she became seriously ill and was finally diagnosed with terminal stomach cancer in 2004. Belinda was by that time my only connection to Wilaipun, because she retired early from teaching as her health grew worse. But because Belinda had maintained that relationship, pointing her also to Christ, the time came when Wilaipun invited me to visit her home again. On this visit, however, Wilaipun had little strength. She was unwilling to use any chemical medicines which meant she had no painkillers, and only herbal remedies to help her even tolerate food. She could hardly eat anything and had lost so much weight. As she laid there on her couch smiling at me through her pain, I asked her if I could ask her a question. She agreed. I asked, "Wilaipun, where will you go when you die?" She looked at me with such a blank look that I was surprised. She replied, "Lisa, Buddhists never think about the future. We always just do what we can to live today. Then tomorrow we do the same. But I will think about that." She then allowed me to pray for her to know Jesus in His truth. A few months, later Belinda informed me that Wilaipun was in the hospital. So I joined Belinda to visit her. Wilaipun's face shone with a joy that could not be explained by any physical relief. She looked at me and said with a big smile, "I told my family I had to come to the Christian hospital. And I'm so delighted that there's a picture of Jesus just outside my door!"[15]

15. Lisa Lehman, e-mail message to author, May 11, 2013.

The Missionary

As the ministry developed at the schools, BJ was given much more latitude to involve the students in creative activities. Each Easter and Christmas, BJ would gather the Christian students at the school (many who attended regular Bible studies with her at lunch time every week), and made displays that told the gospel story. Her English students were also heavily involved in this. In 2007, just after Easter, Jacque, Mitch and I visited BJ in Thailand. We visited the high school where she taught, and the English staff treated us royally! They hosted us for a lunch and proudly escorted us around the school where we could see displays that BJ's classes had made of the gospel story, clearly explaining who Jesus is.

Another missionary colleague in Thailand reflected on her ministry:

It was about walking slowly among the people. It was about

- an open door at the children's home and having children come and play, laugh, tickle, wrestle, and read,
- pizza and bowling parties
- leading times of games as well as times of quiet
- loving to eat som tom, sticky rice and grilled chicken
- visiting the same vendors and allowing Jesus to spill into those relationships
- living consistently in front of the leadership at the local high school so that when the opportunity came to ask if a bible study could be held in her room during the lunch hour, the answer was "yes"
- having high school teachers stay in the room during lunch to "work," only to catch them peeking around the corner, listening to the bible study
- traveling to villages with students
- developing local ministry teams that shared in ministry with teams coming from other countries
- serving as the translator for a new FSC who did not yet know the language
- loving people and sharing Jesus.
- being Jesus with skin on.[16]

---

16. Rolf Kleinfeldt, e-mail message to author, May 12, 2013.

The volunteers were appreciative of the way in which they were included in the ministry in Thailand. Most lived with BJ in her two-bedroom house, or, in the case of a married couple or family, right next door.

> BJ always had time for us all, Abel, myself and our kids. We thought the world of her because she loved with action, time, and understanding. She had so much on her plate all the time . . . the schools, the home with all the children, teams coming all the time, the sponsorship program, us (the volunteers), and a host of problems that always came up. She seemed to be able to handle it all with seeming ease. She rarely seemed stressed or too tired. She gave of herself in a way that just made people at ease. It was a people first lifestyle.
>
> I never felt like I was sufficient for the task we had. I felt like I was lacking most of the time. BJ was so very gifted at everything she was in charge of. I remember doing her laundry for her one day and she was so appreciative and kind about it. I was happy to contribute in any way I could so I often did her laundry after that. It struck me that she was humble enough to have someone hanging her laundry including underwear. She was able to organize almost anyone or any event and still accepted my humble efforts to bless her and she did it with such grace. It touched me.
>
> She always had time for us. We lived next door but it seemed like only one house after a very short time. We never knocked when going for a visit. She had an open door policy. We were always welcomed. It was the hardest thing to adjust to when we got back to Canada after our year in Thailand. People are so formal here. You call before going to see someone and most times you have to make an appointment a week early to see someone as life is so busy here. In Thailand it was pure friendship and acceptance and an attitude of "come in, I'm happy to see you." It blessed us all.
>
> My kids looked up to Belinda very much. She was cool. She was a cool missionary. That is not something you'd expect . . . I will always be thankful for her example to my kids.[17]

From another volunteer:

> We had recently arrived in Chiang Mai, excited to be fulfilling a life-long desire, but we were experiencing serious Culture Shock. After months of preparation, I was feeling very inadequate for my assignment of teaching in a Thai public school. Then we met Belinda and a team from Australia for an evening of Thai food and

---

17. Carol Dizon, e-mail message to author, May 2, 2013.

entertainment. Immediately, Belinda greeted us enthusiastically and with words of encouragement. Throughout the evening she shared tidbits of what I would be doing, and how accepting the teachers would be. By the end of the evening I was feeling much better about our time in Maetang.

In the next two or three weeks, Belinda was very busy with the team from Australia, but she took time to include us in many of their activities and meals. Despite the age difference, we were feeling like partners!

She always showed so much love and acceptance towards the children. Usually by the time I got home from the school, I was ready for some down time, but Belinda's home was a beehive of activity with children coming and going and "helping." She often spent many hours after "work hours" to help high schoolers prepare English assignments. We worked together on Saturday morning English classes for the children living at the Children's Home. One of the most memorable times was conducting a cookie baking session near Christmas time. For most of the middle schoolers it was the first time to make cookies and watch them bake in an oven! Of course Belinda made sure they had flour all over their faces before the session was over![18]

It was Christmas morning, 2004. Christmas wasn't a big thing in Thailand because they are mostly Buddhists. In fact, they didn't even cancel school for Christmas. But for Marlene and me it meant separation from our four daughters for the first holiday. Frankly, we felt lonely. Then I heard a rap on the front door and there was Belinda in her pyjamas. "Would you like to have company for Christmas?" She asked. "Of course," I replied. "Well then I'll go get my presents and we'll have Christmas together." Marlene fixed some cinnamon buns and we had a great time. Later we spent time playing games just like we always did with our family.

Several weeks prior to that, I had received some chocolates for my birthday. Somehow, Belinda always showed up when there was good stuff to eat . . . so she was there. Several Hmong girls from the children's home showed up to share my candy as well. Marlene asked the girls about their native dress and they went to their dorm and came back in their Hmong dresses. I asked the one girl if there were any Christians in her village. Belinda translated what I said into Thai. The older girl then translated it into Hmong. Slowly the translation came back that there were none. In the same

---

18. Marlene Custer, e-mail message to author, May 12, 2013.

arduous way I asked if she was a Christian and she said, "No, but I have wanted to become one." So I, along with Belinda, led her in a prayer to salvation. Then I asked the other girl if she wanted to be a Christian, and she said that she would like to accept Jesus the same way her friend did. And so it happened.[19]

BJ was embraced by a Thai family at MTCH. Very quickly BJ "adopted" a Thai mum. Sasiporn Lawseu (Eido Jasan, her Lahu name) and her children were soon her family in Thailand. Jacque and I were grateful for the Jasan family as they took BJ in and treated her like a daughter/sister. Orathi, Porntip, Upai, Baloon, and Apechai (Sasiporn's children) all became special friends with whom she could have fun, argue, hang out together and generally do what families do together. The connection was deep and meaningful. BJ did not see it as unusual to develop meaningful relationships with young and old alike. It was her experience growing up. It created within her an open, accepting, and embracing spirit that has been an inspiration to many.

Apart from meals with her Thai family, BJ also cultivated friendships with local businesses. One very special relationship was with Nuan, a lady who operated a street side restaurant (dubbed "The Road" by BJ) in Maetang on the main highway. BJ was not a cook. She could cook if she had to, but this was something she did not enjoy. It was logical to eat out as much as she could. The price of a meal was cheap—$1 for a main dish—so it was no chore to journey the five minutes to Nuan's restaurant and enjoy a freshly cooked plate of rice, or noodles, spicy fish or a little chicken. BJ enjoyed Nuan's company and they developed a close relationship.

Rolf Kleinfeldt's comment of BJ about "walking slowly" with the people is apt here. There were times when BJ wondered why she was attending yet another Buddhist ceremony, only to find that in doing so, her relationship with Nuan and her family deepened. It earned her the right to share the Christian story in very tangible and understandable ways. BJ recounts in one of her update newsletters:

> It has been several years now that I have been eating at a restaurant in the local market. It is affectionately known to me, and the numerous volunteers that have eaten with me there as "*The Road*," because the tables are on the footpath and the food is cooked on a small cart that is on the road. The lady that cooks the food at "*The Road*" has gradually, over the years, begun to open up to me. She

---

19. John Custer, e-mail message to author, May 12, 2013.

is not the usual over friendly Thai person. She has a hard exterior and to receive smiles and an acknowledgement of our presence we knew we were becoming "friends." From a smile it has just continued to grow . . . to coming and sitting with us at our table . . . and now she pretty much knows my schedule (e.g. Last week I had forgotten that the next day I would be going to the village but she said to me "I won't see you tomorrow because you are going to the Lahu village again . . . but see you on Saturday, you should be back by then!"). As it is a custom in so many cultures the meal is shared with family . . . and that is exactly what this family that has a rice and a noodle stand and now a Thai salad stand have become.

So, when she invited Heather (one of the volunteers) and I to celebrate Loy Kratong (a Buddhist holiday where kratongs, made out of a banana trunk and leaves and decorated with flowers, incense and candles, are floated down the river to float away one's sins) we knew this was very important for their family and an honour to have been invited. We made plans to be there with her (P'Nuan) that night. We started by letting a large lantern off into sky. As it began to go up she told us to pray. I prayed that we would have a chance to share more about our faith to P'Nuan that very night. We then got the kratongs that she had made for us to float and walked for about 10 mins to an area where there was a celebration happening and an area along the river to float the kratong. On the walk, she asked why we did not want to drink beer on this celebration night and I had the chance to begin to share about my life and my faith. I was able to talk about who I pray to and she had plenty of questions. We talked about the Buddhist festivals and Christian festivals and I had the chance to invite her to Christmas at the Children's Home. We then went and floated the kratongs and enjoyed the very loud music and crazy dancing before walking back to the food stand at the market. On the way back she asked more about our Christmas celebrations and told me to come and pick her and her daughter up for this time. Please pray for this time!! Heather and I also wanted her to come and visit our home around Christmas and see our decorations and lights . . . we mentioned this to her and told her we would come and pick her up at midnight when she closed her stand . . . but she said "Oh no, for a special occasion like this . . . I just won't open my stand up that night!" We are planning on having a little Christmas party with P'Nuan, her daughter Kip and anyone else from their family that wishes to join us. Please pray this will be a meaningful time with intentional conversations![20]

20. Belinda Allder, update newsletter, Dec 2007.

Just a year later BJ shared the circumstances of a significant step in the deepening relationship with Nuan.

> As I sit and write this I think about how far this relationship has come . . . I have to laugh . . . because now Heather and I have even worked as her helpers for her food stall. HAHAHAHA!!! Yes, that's right . . . an American and an Australian (who is definitely not described as a cook!) have been working at "*The Road*." It started over the New Year period as her regular helper went back to her hometown. This is a busy period as many Thai travellers (mostly from Bangkok) are traveling up north for the winter. We got many stares from these tourists who were amazed that foreigners were working at this restaurant. Some even took pics . . . hahahaaha!! We worked hard preparing food, clearing tables, serving meals, collecting the money etc. Heather became the person who cooked all the eggs and I worked on the customer service (Heather thinks I just wanted to talk and not work but I call it customer service!!!). We had a lot of fun . . . and have been called on several times since. . . . Don't worry . . . we aren't getting paid for it or anything . . . just a bit of free food . . . and some free cooking lessons . . . and a lot of fun! We have enjoyed hanging out with P' Nuan, both at the road and around town. We are rarely allowed to go to "*The Road*" and eat and run . . . and if we don't go I am sure to get a phone call.[21]

"Walking slowly" with the people bore fruit. BJ describes Christmas 2007 in Maetang where she and her volunteer English teacher colleague, Heather, had amazing opportunities in their continuing relationship with Nuan. Clearly this took a commitment to spend a lot of time "doing life" and seizing opportunities to share in significant conversations.

> The week leading up to Christmas was VERY busy . . . and it reminded me a lot of what Christmas can be like at "home." (Often here we celebrate Christmas earlier in the month with different groups etc. . . . so the actual date of Dec 25 can be very quiet).
>
> On Dec 19 (Wednesday) we celebrated at the High School. This year our Christian group took more of an active role in leading this activity sponsored by World Vision and supported by a large Christian University. This activity is held in the school hall and attended by *all* students (over 1000 students). The program began with one of our girls introducing the event in English (the English department oversees this activity) and then translated into

---

21. Belinda Allder, update newsletter, Feb 2008.

Thai. I was very proud as Ponthip (Grade 8) spoke clearly and confidently in front of all of her peers. Our Christian group then sang some Christmas carols and then Decha (lecturer at our Nazarene Bible College) gave a short message explaining the real meaning of Christmas. The drama team from Payap University (a Christian University) then entertained the students with songs, and a drama based on The Prodigal Son. The Bible College students gave out Christmas tracts to each student as they left the auditorium. God's Word is going out at Maetang High School!!

Dec 20 (Thursday) PM we began our Christmas carolling travels. We took approximately 40 children carolling from 6pm–midnight around homes of friends, pastors, churches, and missionaries in Chiang Mai. On Friday 21, we did the same thing but around our local Maetang area. Many of those we visited in this area are not Christian, again another time to spread His Word!

Dec 21 (Saturday) was our main party day for the children. We began the day at 8.30 am with an opening prayer from our Director. The party atmosphere was evident as all of the children wore party hats and decorated their tents (in colour groups) that they would sit under for the day. Games were played all morning! I was also excited that P' Nuan the lady from "*The Road*" and her daughter and 2 nephews and another friend came along to participate! A fun time was had by all!! After a special lunch of chicken, rice and soup the team sports competitions begun (volleyball, soccer, and takraw)!

There was barely enough time (or water) for everyone to quickly shower and get ready for the night's activities. We began with a great time of worship together led by some of our older children and a guest speaker brought the message. After this, it was time for the colour groups to put on their shows in a talent show type event. There were plenty of laughs!! (Fashion shows with a difference) Plenty of talent!!! (We definitely do have some super singers, and dancers!!) And plenty of fun!! . . . the night ended just before midnight after the giving of gifts to all of the children. Thank you to all sponsors for making it possible for the children to receive Christmas gifts!! (Their package this year consisted of: soap, shampoo, pens, powder, washing powder, toothpaste, toothbrush, a spoon, a facecloth, body lotion, a drink, and plenty of snacks!).

The next day I was able to celebrate Christmas with my family here (my Thai family) as all of the children had come back from the city for the weekend. We all went out for lunch and a swim. It was a fun time of catching up!

As I said in my last update P' Nuan planned to spend Christmas night with us. Heather (volunteer) and I worked all day (and actually a lot the night before) trying to cook up a storm!! Of course this meant going shopping in the city at the special shop that sells foreign foods. I even found a Christmas ham!!! I was soooooo excited!!! (Heather is a vegetarian so she did not share this excitement. . . . but hey! More for me!!). We had our Thai Christmas carols playing and prepared the last minute things. P' Nuan was very interested in how we cook this foreign food and was puzzled as to why no chilli was used. We realized as we sat down that we had cooked for an army (but hey, it was Christmas!!). P' Nuan of course wanted to take some home for all of her family and neighbours to try this food that the foreigners love to eat. After eating we gave P' Nuan and her daughter presents. They loved them!! One of the things we gave Kip was the Christmas story, in English and Thai (a Children's book). Kip and I sat down and read this together in Thai. P' Nuan told us the parts of the story she already knew and explained that there had been a cartoon on TV about it. Our conversations with P' Nuan continue. She has since told me that she has read parts of the Bible and has even attended church before. She has experienced so much in her life. She continues to let me into her world more and more with each conversation. Please continue to pray for this relationship and family.[22]

"Walking slowly" and the incarnational aspects to BJ's dealing with people are beautifully illustrated in this relationship with Nuan. The story is not yet complete. Twelve months after BJ's death, Jacque and I travelled to Maetang to plant a tree in BJ's honour at the Maetang Tribal Children's Home. Nuan heard of our coming and hosted us at her husband's restaurant the night we arrived, even though his restaurant was supposed to be closed that night. The next night we ate our evening meal at "The Road" with Nuan doing the cooking. It was a special moment. Nuan was present for the simple ceremony where we acknowledged BJ's contribution to Nazarene ministry in Thailand. We loved having her as an active participant in remembering BJ's impact on all our lives. We were able to meet Nuan's daughter and husband, and we pray that the seeds planted, the sense of belonging that BJ nurtured with Nuan between her family and ours, and the gentle wooing of God's Holy Spirit will continue in Nuan's life. Greater things are yet to come!

---

22. Belinda Allder, update newsletter, Feb 2008.

The Missionary

A very useful tool that the South East Asia Field provided for BJ while at Maetang was an old twelve-seater Toyota van. I am not sure how long it had been with the Nazarene mission, but it testified to a hard life. BJ was no mechanic. She understood vehicles to be no more than means to an end—the way to connect to more people! Niceties such as regular maintenance, and even regular checks of water and oil, were never on her horizon. Thankfully she always appeared to have people around her who were much more in tune with these practicalities. Eventually the old white bus expired, and BJ was given a nice blue pickup truck. In some countries this would have restricted what BJ could do to transport people around—but not in Thailand. It was common to see the back loaded with people as BJ would transport as many people as possible to the next exciting activity. It was also a perfect vehicle for the Songkran Festival held each April for Thai New Year. This is a water festival, which, in Chiang Mai and surrounding areas, is an excuse to have three days of water "fights"! Anyone walking outside is fair game to be doused with water (often iced water!) as a "blessing" for the New Year. Pickup trucks loaded with people, tubs of water, buckets and water pistols travel the streets and douse each other (and everybody else) with water. It is a time of great fun and laughter as well as a time to cool off from the oppressive humidity. BJ loved that time!

BJ was thankful for a reliable vehicle! I remember being with her in Maetang when she was complaining about having no air conditioning in her old bus—a real challenge in very hot and humid Thailand. I suggested we go to the local mechanic in Maetang and get it repaired (I was willing to pay!). However it wasn't just a matter of going down and getting it done. Despite her amazing facility with the language, she had very little vocabulary that involved mechanics and air conditioning. How do you describe what the problem is? Well we tried anyway. It is interesting what challenges come the way of missionaries in very different contexts to their own. However, BJ's biggest complaint with her nice "new" blue truck was that no one recognised her driving around for a time. Previously, there would be people in Maetang tooting their horns or waving greetings as she past. It seems that "everyone" knew BJ and the old white bus! As you can imagine, it didn't take long before the blue truck was recognised just as quickly. Driving the roads to villages in the hills of Thailand is always a challenge, but especially so in an unreliable, underpowered, overfull white bus! The blue truck was a real blessing. When BJ returned home for medical treatment she missed having her truck!

Over time, BJ's ministry activities extended far beyond the borders of the Maetang Tribal Children's home and its surrounding areas. From her times in Bangkok in language school and meetings with missionary colleagues, BJ had established good working relationships with many in the church there. She was active in youth camps and discipleship training in and around Thailand. She was appointed South East Asia Field Nazarene Youth International (NYI) coordinator and began to be involved in youth camps and leadership development retreats in Thailand, Vietnam and elsewhere in South East Asia. Her travels took her to the Philippines, Singapore, South Africa, and the United States working with youth. Her facility with the Thai language and her good relational connections with the youth of South East Asia made her a logical choice to be translator and chaperone for various trips to the Philippines and other countries for conferences. Broadening young people's horizons to catch a global perspective of what God is doing was a part of BJ's agenda. These trips were life changing for many young people as they captured the enthusiasm and joy of serving God in ways similar to BJ. She was an inspiration and a challenge to, what she considered to be, fellow sojourners.

> A highlight for April was my trip to Vietnam. This was a trip to go in and meet the youth of the church there!! And, what a good group it is!! They took me on an outing on my first day there. Approx. 40 people loaded onto a bus and headed to a beach and Monkey Island. I was able to run the games for them . . . and I think some of them are still getting massages to recover . . . oops!!! (Hopefully they will have me back . . .). On the Sunday we started with Sunday School at 7.30 (in which I shared) and then church at 9.30 (again I shared). After the service there was a time to pray to accept Christ and 6 young girls who have been in a small Bible Study prayed to accept Christ! It was sooooo neat to be a part of that!! That same week one of the young girls there got a Visa to go to study in Korea at Korean Nazarene University. It was a miracle to get this visa without any "additional" money being paid!!! Praise God!! Please pray for Bich Phuong as this is her first time out of the country and she will be studying in her 3rd language (Korean). After church we fellowshipped over lunch and rested before having some more fun of games with the young people. Vietnam is certainly a beautiful place and God is moving!![23]

---

23. Belinda Allder, update newsletter, May 2008.

The energy expended, and the desire to be involved in everything was truly exhausting to those who did not have the physical stamina or passion that BJ had. As volunteers, Peter and Leanne mentioned in their reflections previously:

> We find ourselves trying to do things and look at situations the way you do. We exhaust people in ways that we never did before.[24]

Perhaps the best way to pull together the strands of BJ's remarkable ministry is by way of reflections from another of the volunteers who worked with BJ. Phil Cellich, now a medical doctor in Australia, was part of the youth group in Birrong, part of a Youth in Mission trip to Thailand, and then a volunteer for over twelve months in Thailand with BJ.

> As I write this, it is almost 10 years since BJ came back to her home church at Birrong, following her initial 12 month NIVS (Nazarenes in Volunteer Service) assignment in Maetang, and shared with us about her ministry there and her passion for reaching out to the people of Thailand. So that means it is also almost 10 years since God first spoke to me about missions and ministering to those less fortunate in places less comfortable. God used BJ's passion to speak strongly to my spirit, and although I am still unsure of the details of God's call on my life, I continue to seek Him, and remain on the path He set me on all those years ago.
>
> That was not the first time that God had reached out to me through BJ—in fact, in numerous ways, BJ was instrumental in my coming to know Christ in the first place—but it was certainly one of the clearest, most direct, most life-changing times that God has spoken to me to date. It resulted in my being part of a "Youth in Mission" team to Thailand in 2004, and then later embarking on my own NIVS assignment at Maetang. Despite the ups and downs I have experienced since then, I still thank God for the way He used BJ in that moment, and the way He spoke to me in the time that followed. To this day I am seeking to fulfil that call.
>
> I remember the first time I touched down in the strange new land of Chiang Mai, Thailand. Everything was new and uncertain. The smells, sights and sounds were so different to anything I had experienced before. I didn't know the language, or how to get from one place to another. In hindsight it could have been such an intimidating experience, but I felt so confident because we had BJ leading us. I can't imagine what it must have been like the first time BJ went to Thailand for her NIVS assignment, without

24. Peter Clarke and Leanne Clarke, BJ memorial service eulogy, Feb 24, 2012.

the benefit of having someone familiar who had gone before. It became a recurring theme for me that BJ was always there to encourage me, having been there before. That was always one of her gifts—supporting, encouraging, inspiring. Not only did she do it for me, time and again, but also for countless others, especially the many volunteers that she hosted through Maetang.

I will never forget our trip into the mountains to visit the people of Doi Fa Pa—thousands of kilometres from home, headed to an unknown remote location, with no way of contacting "civilisation." It was my first youth in mission assignment, and the team, led by BJ, had hopped in the back of the ute, along with a couple of ring-ins, with our trusty driver, Mee Chai, at the wheel. There had been more rain than expected, and the steep, windy dirt road through the mountains had turned to mud. As the ute slid and slipped along, precariously close to the shear drop into the valley below, with none of the safety barriers that you would expect on a similarly treacherous road at home, BJ was still able to instil confidence in us, despite her own fear and uncertainty. It was her faith that did it, and although we all shared the same faith, somehow hers was so much more evident than anyone else's. Needless to say, God protected us and we all survived. What an amazing experience it was, being one of the most remote villages we were able to visit, meeting with the beautiful people, feeling that God was somehow closer now that the hustle and bustle of modern life had been stripped away. We hoped that we had been an encouragement in some small way to the church in Doi Fa Pa, but God had certainly been working in each of us on the team. If it wasn't for BJ's leadership and faith, I wonder whether that trip would ever have happened.

In addition to using BJ as an example of what faith in action looks like, God also used her to teach me what a real relationship with God is, including the importance of regular communication with Him through prayer and bible reading. It seemed natural for BJ. Not to say that it was always easy for her, or that there weren't times when she didn't feel like it, but more that, for her, it was just a given that God was part of our everyday lives. Coming from a largely atheist family background, this was new for me. The following was part of an email that I sent to BJ quite a number of years ago now, shortly after I had returned to Australia following my first YIM assignment. Although it is somewhat embarrassing looking back on it, it is nothing if not genuine, and I think it speaks of the impact that Belinda had on my relationship with God.

The Missionary

"Remember, I'm praying for you every day. And that's a lot for me, you know . . . Actually, I think I have you to thank for that. Before Thailand my prayer life was hopeless. Sometimes, I could count the number of prayers in a week on one hand. But, through you, and the Thailand trip, God reminded me what it is to have a real relationship with Him. Since I've been back I've managed to have a devotion time most mornings, and I find myself talking to God multiple times per day . . . This all might sound a little . . . juvenile . . . but I guess that's what my relationship with God was like. Anyway, cutting a long story short, thanks for your help, whether you knew you gave it or not. And now you can count on my prayers daily."

BJ was always a people person. During my years in Thailand, as I became better acquainted with the language and culture, and as I became more and more aware of the politics and the uglier side of the communities in which BJ worked, I never heard a negative word spoken about her. In any community there are people with differing opinions, and people that rub others up the wrong way, and it is inevitable that someone won't like the way something is being done. Even still, in Thailand, I never saw any evidence of this directed toward BJ. People respected her. Most people loved her. I believe they saw something of God's love and grace in her. She gave what she had, but wasn't after something in return. I wish I could have been more like that. That's yet another thing I will take with me, and strive for in the time I have left.

As part of her caring and her giving, BJ really "filled in the gaps" at the Children's Home. If something needed doing and wasn't getting done, or if someone was needed to fill a certain role, BJ would often step up. This ranged from the very official—being the guest of honour at community events, or organising district level educational activities—to the very informal—being a mum or a big sister to a child that was going through a tough time. I've taken the liberty of listing out some of these roles, at least the ones I observed her fulfilling. As you'll see, some are listed in light-hearted fond reflection, and some on a more serious note, marking great sacrifice. I'm sure different people will identify more with BJ in some roles than others, but I believe that all are accurate, and all meant with the utmost respect. These roles included: teacher, friend, leader, tour guide, photographer, negotiator, human resources coordinator, cultural liaison officer, ambassador, translator, interpreter, mum, missionary, counsellor, judge, event coordinator, treasurer, traveller, peacemaker, mediator, driver, pastor, gift giver, mentor, host, karaoke star, advocate, bargain hunter, role model, model, drama queen, librarian, project manager, careers advisor, big sister, disciple-maker, and of course, Christ-like disciple. This list could go on and on, and much could be written about each of these roles in turn. While it would be easy to light-heartedly skim through this list as it evokes memories of this or that time with BJ, I think it is also important to remember that this list of roles also came with great stress and pressure for BJ. She would joke about being mum, or tour guide, and she would always do it with a smile and with love, but sometimes I think the responsibility weighed heavily on her. In the laid-back, it's-someone-else's-problem culture of much of the community in which BJ lived and worked, it would have been so easy to have done so much less. It is a credit to BJ, and a testament to the God working within her, that she didn't.

BJ loved to enjoy life, and help others enjoy life too. It was her idea to start the tradition of monthly birthday outings for all the Children's Home kids that had their birthday that month. This was always to somewhere special, like Mok Fa waterfall or tenpin bowling in the city, and was a real treat and moment of real enjoyment for all the kids. BJ was the driving force behind many of these sorts of activities, and unfortunately, as was often the case, if BJ wasn't around, these things would fall by the wayside. The annual Christmas celebration, with special food for the day, activities, competitions and sports, and the annual Christmas "pageant," was another example of a touch of excitement and enjoyment for the kids, driven by BJ. But this didn't end with the Children's Home kids. Whoever you were, BJ had a way of making you feel as though you were important to her. She was always willing to make time for a coffee and a chat. She saw the importance of building relationships and giving people moments of joy through activities that were "just for fun." Whether it was taking some time out to show volunteers around the tourist attractions of Bangkok, or organizing makeup evenings for the ladies at the Children's Home, or even over a cup of coffee or plate of som tam and sticky rice, BJ took the time to connect with people. She even used to get involved in the city-wide water fights of the Songkran festival, driving her ute into the thick of the fights around the central city moat. I certainly never saw any other missionaries doing anything of the sort, and it meant that she developed deeper, more impacting relationships with the people in her community, again, of the sort that I didn't see other missionaries achieving.

BJ was gifted with practical skills and abilities that often went under-recognised. BJ's communication skills deserve particular attention. This includes her Thai language skills. I feel perhaps

The Missionary

particularly qualified to comment on her language skills, having shared a similar linguistic background (Western Sydney English), and having attempted to attain similar proficiency in the Thai language. BJ's ability and willingness to communicate in Thai was inspiring. By the end of my time in Thailand I feel that my grasp of more formal and technical Thai vocabulary may have even slightly exceeded BJ's, having had the benefit of living in the city and mixing with a greater number of more highly educated Thai people. But this counted for nothing when it came to communicating with people, especially in a church / ministry setting. BJ's ability to preach in Thai, and to interpret sermons or testimonies from Thai to English or English to Thai was phenomenal, and given the cultural environment in which she worked, this would often be required with very little notice. This was clearly a gift that went beyond just language. When BJ met with Lahu people, particularly those who lived in the mountains, whose first language was not Thai, her ability to communicate shone through. It was in this environment that I believe she was more effective even than a native Thai speaker would have been.

I also remember just the stuff of everyday life. Trips to Mae Malai, the nearest town centre, for dinner at "the road," or later night trips for those deep fried doughnut-like things with the sweet green dipping sauce (I'm not sure that we ever worked out quite what those things were!). Devotion times were invariably "driven" by BJ; preparing lesson plans; crazy large group bible study/Sunday school activities with way too many kids to keep under any sort of control or order; singing worship songs in the van; taking the shortcut to school, past the temple, avoiding the mud and occasionally the water buffalo, over the dodgy bridge; special dinners at Mae Ngat dam where we ordered the whole fish; having the living room floor littered with children; listening to problems and offering advice; bargain hunting at the Walking Street market; cruising in the van with the windows down and "Casting Crowns" blaring—I can't listen to "Who am I?" by Casting Crowns without thinking of those times. I fear that this might not make particularly interesting reading for those that didn't have the chance to go there and share some of these experiences, but the fact is that this was life. And it was through these everyday moments that Belinda ministered most effectively. It wasn't through preaching God's word in a second language, although she certainly did that. It wasn't through showing the Jesus film, although she was involved in that too. It was through who she was in the moments of everyday life. It was through her taking an opportunity for a conversation, or being available to listen. This is not to look down upon any of those other methods or tools for ministry, but simply to say this is how God reached out to people through BJ's life.

But I wouldn't be being honest if I left it at that, sounding as though life was always pleasant and easy and free from worry and stress and pressure. It wasn't. There were times when I know BJ felt out of her depth with the level of responsibility sometimes thrust upon her. The mission field can be a lonely place, even when you're surrounded by people—especially for BJ who was often the sole missionary working at a remote location. No one really understands what it's like, not people at home or local friends and colleagues—nowhere and everywhere is home. BJ also often found herself in the middle of conflicts and issues happening between church leaders and the Children's Home. As with any organization made up of fallible human beings with sometimes different goals and agendas, there were politics at play which BJ had to negotiate. The difference for her, though, was that she was doing this in another country, away from the usual supports of family and community, and with sometimes unrealistic expectations from others about what her role should be and how much power she had to change things. She felt trapped between those that insistently asked her to make changes that were beyond her control, and those that actually had the power to change things but were either unwilling or unsure about the wisdom of making such changes. To her credit, BJ didn't allow this tension behind the scenes to impact on her ministry with the children at the Children's Home and the people of the local community. In fact, when things were at their most unstable, despite feeling out of her depth, I believe that it was often BJ that held things together and ensured that the ministry of the Children's Home continued into the future.

I am sorry to say that, while volunteering at Maetang, I personally contributed to the worry, pressure and stress that Belinda faced. In one of the biggest mistakes of my life, I compromised both my NIVS assignment and my relationship with Belinda in one fell swoop. This is not the place for the details of the mistakes I made, but suffice to say that out of something initially innocent grew something inappropriate, all of which put BJ in a very difficult position. To this day, I regret some of the decisions I made at the time, and the heartache I caused Belinda, but I am continually amazed as I reflect on the lack of judgement that I felt from her, and the forgiveness that I received. When I returned to Thailand, no longer as a volunteer with the church, I made contact with BJ by email, and this was part of her reply:

"Despite the circumstances, not a lot has changed. You are still the Phil Cellich I grew up with, my mate from home, my mate from Birrong. You know my number."

This blot on my record wouldn't be worth mentioning, except that it serves to highlight BJ's love, grace and forgiveness. I pray that I can one day attain to her example.

BJ wore her heart on her sleeve. This led to her crying almost every time she gave her testimony (to which I would roll my eyes, and she would laugh)! But her tears were genuine, triggered by a keen sense of God's presence, leading, and protection in her life. It was this genuineness and openness that allowed her to communicate with people so effectively, and made so many people love her. The kids at the Children's Home certainly loved her, especially the little ones. It was not uncommon to see kids chasing after her van to see her upon her return to the Children's Home. BJ, in her openness and thoughtfulness, would often write little letters or notes to people, to encourage them, to express thanks, to clear the air, or to share a bible verse. BJ was wonderfully gifted at encouraging. Importantly, this never felt like the forced, fake encouragement that you can get sometimes when someone is obviously really struggling to find something positive to say. BJ was always so genuine that you'd really start to believe what she said about you. Now, don't get me wrong, BJ was a real bandit (to use some language from the youth group days) for super-cheesy notes, letters, quotes, and finding the cheesiest sounding bible verses possible, but somehow, when it came from her it was so genuine—with such a truth and honesty about it. I was the recipient of so many encouraging notes, cards, letters, phone calls, MSN chats over the years, but I am aware of her doing the same for so many others. It was this people-focus, combined with her genuineness and vulnerability that allowed her to impact so many lives for Christ.[25]

We have this treasure in clay jars, so that it may be made clear that this extraordinary power belongs to God and does not come from us. We are afflicted in every way, but not crushed; perplexed, but not driven to despair; persecuted, but not forsaken; struck down, but not destroyed; always carrying in the body the death of Jesus, so that the life of Jesus may be made visible in our mortal flesh. (2 Cor 4:7–11 NRSV)

---

25. Phil Cellich, e-mail message to author, May 15, 2013.

Chapter 4

Doing Life

BJ WAS GIFTED IN discipling others into a vital, living faith in Jesus Christ. Naturally, although quite intentionally, she gathered groups around her for "doing life," and learning to be authentic in their walk with Jesus. While in Brisbane undergoing cancer treatment, BJ soon gathered old and new friends around her with whom she met regularly (usually weekly) for "doing life."[1] These young ladies became an amazing support for BJ through her two and a half years of illness. They studied God's Word together, prayed together, played together, embraced each other's families, and when illness dominated BJ's life, they were there to assist. They would do "girlie weekends," take a turn at spending the day with BJ during her regular chemo sessions, and share lots of their family times together. Husbands of the ladies were amazingly supportive as they became part of the wider extended discipleship family group. BJ was "God mother" to each of their children and she took this task seriously. She remembered their children's birthdays, celebrated school successes and sporting achievements, and ensured that each of the children had a Bible that she had bought and addressed to each one personally.

> Our Bible study group!! I praise God this is happening. It is a blessing for me to have this kind of thing and develop relationships. It is a highlight of my week. Great friends and we get to grow closer to God together.[2]

> Thank God for our Bible study last night. So great when all the girls are there!!—and the study was dealing with loneliness, health,

---

1. The core group consisted of Mel Good, Mariko Fulton, Melissa McCray (her cousin), and Nakari Pratt. Others from time to time joined the group or BJ met with individual people regularly apart from this group.
2. BJ diary, Feb 3, 2010.

unemployment, marital issues—it covered all of us. I think it really spoke to all of us.[3]

In BJ's "Thank You" diary, she mentions each of these girls by name on several occasions. Here is just a sample:

Melinda

Thanx Lord for Mel. I am so blessed to have met her on that first day of university—so blessed that we really connected!!! I don't know what life would be like without her. She is my companion. She is my best friend who truly knows me! She is my encouragement. I know I have a friend for life in her—now Jim, Jeremiah and Ben too!!! Words cannot express how thankful I am![4]

Thank you God for my awesome best friend Mel! I had a shocker emotional day and got all teary—just couldn't stop. Mel came up and just hung out with me—she listened, she understood. I am so grateful for her friendship and love—even when I am carrying on and being emotional and dumb!![5]

Melissa

I thank God for my cousin and our relationship! I thank God she has been coming to the Bible study group and seems so relaxed to be there. I thank God she is so involved. I thank God for her openness and recognising God in her life.[6]

I thank God that I am hanging with the McCrays—just what I needed! Having the kids fight over me (ha ha!). Makes me feel loved.[7]

---

3. Ibid., June 22, 2011.
4. Ibid., Aug 16, 2010.
5. Ibid., Sept 12, 2010.
6. Ibid., Feb 17, 2011.
7. Ibid., June 12, 2011.

Mariko (Muzzy)

Muzz!! Today is her birthday and we went to Toowoomba to stay with her family. It was really a fun time!! I thank God for this new friend that I feel I have grown so close to. Bless her heaps this day.[8]

Sydney!!! Great time walking all over Sydney with Muzzy! I thank God for a friend to take and spend time with. I thank God I was well enough to make the trip. Thanx God for the safe travels and not getting lost etc. Beautiful blue sky day to go on the ferry. Gotta love Sydney—best city in the world!! And it was looking spectacular today.[9]

Nakari

When I went into hospital to have my stent put in Karz (Nakari), Mel and Andrea did a makeover of my room. It is AMAZING!! They gave *so* much to do that for me. I have just felt so loved—it is *so* humbling. Who am I that people would do all of this??[10]

I thank God for Nakari's idea for Ministry of food! Just love the idea but also how Nakari is taking some leadership. It shows me that she loves our group—I am so happy to see how this group is really growing together and with God.[11]

In hospital, but finally in the ward after 13 hours in emergency. I thank God for my own room. I thank God that I don't feel too bad. I thank God for great friends visiting (tonite Mel and Karz came) and great friends calling, texting etc.[12]

Nakari! Today is her birthday! I thank God for this beautiful "lifetime" friend. I thank you Lord for how our friendship has grown over this past year or so! Bless her this day!![13]

---

8. Ibid., May 22, 2010.
9. Ibid., Jan 28, 2011.
10. Ibid., Dec 1, 2009.
11. Ibid., July 6, 2010.
12. Ibid., Apr 12, 2011.
13. Ibid., June 23, 2011.

Doing Life

Soon after her diagnosis the girls (under the creative inspiration of Nakari) gained access to her bedroom while BJ was still in hospital. They decorated it in very tasteful but amazing ways. The ceiling was covered with stars that illuminated at night, reminding BJ of her life theme of serving God "under his sky"; the wall hangings reminded her of Thailand, and practical additions were made to the room to make it comfortable during the long, often sleepless, nights. In her last days, many people came to visit her. According to Mitch, our younger son, 253 different people passed through our doors in the last month of BJ's life. That meant many cups of tea and coffee, snacks, etc., as many returned to visit several times. It was the discipleship girls who helped with some of the hospitality that fell to us on frequent occasions. At the latter stages Mariko took a few days off work and was front door greeter and tea maker. Mel was there in BJ's darker moments to be a listening ear, encourager and friend. These were special times for Belinda who was constantly encouraged and energised by her many visitors.

We remember the first time in conversation with the oncologist when BJ noticed other patients walking around with scarves covering bald heads from hair loss. She was nervous and a little frightened by the sight. She realised that her own, thick beautiful hair may well be lost through the treatment time. Her friends, along with what was to be her discipleship girls, picked up on this concern and planned a "shave our hair day." They joined BJ in losing (shaving) their hair. After church one Sunday afternoon, a number of her friends, including her brother Mitch (who had long hair himself!) gathered at our home to shave each other's hair. The event was fun with lots of laughter and it seemed that hair loss was no big deal after all. Emblazoned on the T-shirt BJ wore that day were the words, "Never, never, never, give up!" Thank the Lord for friends who identified with BJ enough to join her journey in this symbolic way!

"Doing life together" was an intentional principle for her, and not just a happy accident. She loved to socialise and was often dubbed a "social butterfly." If that term was meant to imply that she was superficial, it was a wrong designation. However, she did love to socialise with many people, but be authentic with them. She had an amazingly large network of friends.

A sermon that she preached on a number of occasions, based upon Luke 1:39–56, gives further expression to importance of community living.

> The story of Mary is so well known. We especially all turn to think of her at Christmas time. We think about how she was the mother

of Jesus. We think about how the angel spoke to her and how she travelled that long distance to Bethlehem on the donkey only to be told "No Room." We think about how she gave birth to Jesus in a stable and cradled him in a manger. This is probably one of the most well-known stories about Christianity. We know it so well that sometimes we become complacent about it. We just accept the story without really thinking about the characters involved. Yes, the birth of Jesus is the main part of the story but let's stop and think about the others involved. I want us to think about Mary. Each Christmas, I am reminded of the strong faith that she had. First, to even be in tune to be spoken to by an angel and understand and accept what was being asked of her. And then to go through with a pregnancy that the world around her could not understand. To experience the judging eyes as she walked down the street, to have to go home and explain such a thing to her parents (what father of a teenage daughter is going to take the angel story?!?!) . . .

And that's all before the birth . . . *not* to mention the life ahead of her as she mothers the Messiah.

Do we just think that back and presume people were different then? Do we think that these things were normal and she could just handle the situation . . . like they were some extra powerful humans that were back in Bible times . . . ?!?! No, these people are regular human beings . . . with fears, feelings, family, communities, cultural pulls . . . *just like us*!

Mary is told by the angel Gabriel that she is going to mother the Messiah of the world, Jesus. She is told that the Holy Spirit will come upon her and she will become pregnant. *Wow*! Imagine that for an experience . . . what would her Facebook status be after that?!?!

Mary believed! And then we come to this scripture . . . Luke 1:39–56

Mary went straight to Elizabeth. We can work out that it was almost straight away by knowing that Elizabeth was 6 months pregnant when the angel told Mary, and Mary stayed with Elizabeth 3 months . . . she must have left Elizabeth just before the birth of John. And it was not a rash decision to just go down the road and visit her cousin. The town was 80–100 miles away. This would have taken her 3 or 4 days. Definitely not just a pop in next door! But Mary went . . .

Mary went straight to Elizabeth—an older woman . . . perhaps a bit like a mentor. She knew she needed that time. I am sure Mary found great comfort in Elizabeth who understood her. She just "got it." Even from the moment she greeted Mary—v. 41–42

"When Elizabeth heard Mary's greeting, the baby leaped in her womb, and Elizabeth was filled with the Holy Spirit. In a loud voice she exclaimed: "Blessed are you among women, and blessed is the child you will bear!" That must have just encouraged Mary so much, to know that Elizabeth got it, to know that Elizabeth fully understood her and this unusual situation. As Christians living in the world—perhaps you have experienced this . . . or have longed for this . . . someone who just "gets you." That's where the community of faith comes in. We are to be that to each other. We are to be there for each other in real life! We are to help each other through the hard times, the good times, build each other up, hold each other accountable. As it says in Hebrews 10:24–25:

> And let us consider how we may spur one another on toward love and good deeds. Let us not give up meeting together, as some are in the habit of doing, but let us encourage one another—and all the more as you see the Day approaching.

Mary must have been encouraged also as the "call" was confirmed. The things the angel had spoken to Elizabeth too. Mary's actions and response showed that she believed the angel but this must have been a double reassurance as Elizabeth confirmed it all.

What did they do during these 3 months?? Luke doesn't mention all that these cousins got up to but I would love to have been there. I am sure they had the girly chats. I am sure they shared pregnancy stories and advice. This was exciting and new for both of them although Elizabeth was 6 months ahead.

I think they also spent a lot of time in prayer together. What a power source when we can be in prayer together!

I am also sure they spent time in the scriptures. Mary's "Magnificat," which is the song here in verses 46–55, shows her understanding of the scriptures and that she was a student of the Word. She was probably pondering stories such as Hannah as she travelled to see Elizabeth.

Mary and Elizabeth needed this time as they encouraged each other, and drew strength from each other and from Him. This was a time that they would look back on and cling to as trouble came. As we know the stories of these two women we know that they experienced difficult times after this encounter (not to mention the child birth alone . . . as I'm sure those who have gone through can testify to) . . . but also . . . Elizabeth was soon to lose her husband and then not long after that her own life. She was only a mother for a short time. And Mary would soon experience the death of her son . . . Jesus. Mary felt this deeply and walked with her son . . .

even to the cross. As Simeon predicted when they presented Jesus in the temple as a boy . . . He said to Mary "This child is destined to cause the falling and rising of many in Israel, and to be a sign that will be spoken against, so that the thoughts of many hearts will be revealed. And a sword will pierce your own soul too." (Luke 2:34-35) Mary had all that to come!

This kind of relationship, like Mary and Elizabeth had, is crucial as we journey in our Christian lives! It is so important to have people who know you well, who "get you," who you can pray with, who you can grow with, and to whom you can be accountable.

As I have been living here in Australia the past year I have experienced something of this sort. It was not my intention to be here for this year. But God has placed Marys and Elizabeth's in my life. This time has been a time of encouragement and a time to "fill up" before going into the unknown future. The girls in my Bible Study have all been a part of my life (well most of them) for several years (2 of them I have known all my life!) . . . but we have never experienced a time of living together in the same city for a length of time. And here we find ourselves, all for very different reasons—5 girls—living here in Brisbane, and journeying life together. It has been a deeply spiritual time as we have gotten into God's Word together, as we have prayed together, shared life's struggles and life's joys together. We are preparing for the unknown futures . . . we know there are tough days ahead, now is the time to prepare! And what a joy that God has given us others to prepare with, others that "get it." Others that "get us"; that understand us.

Are we looking for relationships that will encourage us and allow us time to "fill up," to get ready to face the future? As Mary sought out Elizabeth I am sure this time was not just an encouragement for Mary, but also for Elizabeth. It is a mutual relationship.

Are we being Marys? Are we seeking out older, mature Christians to learn from, to be mentored by? Are we allowing ourselves to be vulnerable? Are we allowing others to help shape us and develop us? Or are we being unteachable and thinking that we are ok on our own? That we know it all? Despite the fact that the angel had spoken to Mary; that Mary was chosen to carry the Saviour; that Mary was well immersed in the scriptures . . . she did not hold this attitude. She did not consider herself "above it" but humbled herself before Elizabeth. Mary was not seeking a title for herself. I am not saying that we hold Mary in a high light, (as some faiths believe we should) . . . but just that we should learn from her selfless faith and Godly obedience. We can also learn from her about Christian community.

Are we being Elizabeths? Are we encouraging others in the faith? Are we affirming others in their call? Or are we letting our "Aussie" culture take over and exhibiting the "tall poppy syndrome"? Elizabeth did not react in jealousy at all! Are we spending time building others up?

In Phil 2:1–4 we read:

> If you have any encouragement from being united with Christ, if any comfort from his love, if any fellowship from the Spirit, if any tenderness and compassion, then make my joy complete by being likeminded, having the same love, being one in spirit and purpose. Do nothing out of selfish ambition or vain conceit, but in humility consider others better than yourselves. Each of you should look not only to your own interests, but also to the interests of others.

The "if" here is really "since." It is since we have been united with Christ, have received comfort from his love, and fellowship from the Spirit that we want to be united with our fellow brother and sister in Christ. We are called to humble ourselves and live in community. It is as He has encouraged us that we must be an encouragement to others! It is our response from all that Christ has done for us, the *encouragement* that is to our lives . . . that we will in turn want to encourage others. If we become so inward thinking that we lose sight of all that Christ has done for us, and make things about *us* . . . then we lose the motivation, the driving force, the natural pull to *encouragement* . . . and true community is lost.

As Paul has said in Romans 1:11–12:

> I long to see you, so that I may impart to you some spiritual gift to make you strong- that is, you and I may be mutually encouraged by each other's faith.

May that be the experience we have with our fellow brothers and sisters in Christ. May we be like Mary and seek out that mentor in the faith. May we be like Elizabeth and be an encouragement to others. May we be selfless as we put the needs of others before our own. May we see God in others and let them know it. May we take encouragement from others and "fill up" as we prepare for the "trouble" ahead, the unknown future. May we seek to live in true community!

As it says in 1 Thess 5:11

> Therefore encourage one another and build each other up, just as you are doing.

> How well do you know the people in your church? How well do you know the people in your faith community? Make a point of getting to know them *today*! Take the time to get to know them. Take time to enter their worlds. Take time to encourage them. Take time to walk life with them! Really walk life . . . not just a polite smile as you enter church.
> . . . and who knows . . . you may just be encouraged yourself.
> May you be encouraged and be an encouragement to others.[14]

In the last few weeks of BJ's life she was too ill to attend church, so we planned church at home. Times of corporate worship were a high priority with BJ. There was always a small group of friends who would join us for special moments of worship together. We treasure those moments as a family. On Sunday February 5, just ten days before her passing, BJ delivered her last sermon in our home church, based upon the sermon just quoted. She was very aware that she had only days left to share these precious moments of corporate worship with friends. A small group of those she had discipled in Sydney travelled to Brisbane for the day to spend time with her. These are the final words of that sermon:

> It wasn't my plan to be here. Brisbane has never been home and I have never really wanted it to be . . . But God just had amazing ways of having my closest friends from Sydney—from my whole life really—be here at this time and in this place. We have never been able to be together like this for so long—and to be able to meet every day and be so close—what a blessing that has been. We decided to have English Bible study, which for me I had not had for so long. And to have my cousin part of that—we had never lived in the same city—and to be brave enough to ask her to be a part of that Bible study. To see the journey she has been on for the last two years has been an encouragement to me—and to have Nakari be part of it too! This is just a part of "here"—the network of support has been much larger than that.
>
> We need to as Christians not just to go to church and shut ourselves off to those that are just right there. We can just open ourselves and it is just so amazing when we can walk together. It just doesn't have to be the big D & Ms (*"deep and meaningfuls"*) or the big "get the Bible out" and study from some Scripture, but live life together and be real. And that's what I see in Mary

---

14. Belinda Allder, unpublished sermon written as part of her master of arts studies at NTC, Brisbane. She had the opportunity to preach this is in several places in Australia through 2011.

and Elizabeth as they shared together. I am sure they would have cried a lot. They had these scary lives in front of them and nobody else really understood. But they "got it." And we need to be with people who just "get us." Sure we need to be in the world and have non-Christian friends and be able to share that love, but we need refuelling too and we need to be with people who "get us." We can share the horrible stuff as well as the good stuff to get us by. Because that is what God has given us. We are not supposed to do this by ourselves.

I just want to encourage you guys to find those friends—they're more than friendships. They are people to really walk with and share with. It is hard to open up to people. I think that is our problem. We just want to keep it to ourselves and we think, "O my problems—that big!" But really that is life's stuff. And everyone has stuff—no matter how small or big. We just need to be encouraged to walk the walk together because we can't do it by ourselves. I think that in our churches we can begin to do that, and actually take a little notice of who is sitting in the pew around us and not just on Sundays. Actually think about their lives and the things they are going through each day—even just a chat. I really believe we would develop who we are as the people of God and strengthen us.

This passage has kept me going over the past two years—not just the Christmas part but Mary and Elizabeth having such a companionship. They had scary things coming up in their lives. Elizabeth was about to lose her husband. She was old and there was so much ahead of her. And Mary had to walk with her son to the cross. We know how close she was to Him. They didn't know but they had to refuel because something was ahead and they had to be ready for it. We know trouble is coming. Are we prepared for it? Are we ready for it? So they took that time out together. I am sure they read Scripture together. I am sure they prayed together. I am sure they cried together and laughed together as well. That's real life. Seeking out other people, but not only us seeking others but being open to let others into our lives, no matter how old or young we are. Where we are at sometimes we think, "O that person is much more spiritual than me or whatever." But as we have learned with our own group, we are all the same. It doesn't matter how long we have been walking with God or not, we need each other. . . . That is my greatest fear for all you guys over the next few weeks or months, that you will drop off (*following Jesus*). Just hold each other up and help each other through. Know that this is the blessing we have as Christians—we do have each other. And the greater blessing that we will see each other again. But in the meantime we have each other to continue on.

Prayer: Lord I just thank you for your Word and that it speaks to us afresh each day. I thank you for the promises; I thank you for encouragement and leading. I also want to thank you for these people who are with me right now. I just thank you for their support. I thank you Lord that they have been holding me up. There is nothing that I can do, but it is through the support of others—they continue to hold me up and continue to give me strength and energy for each day. And I thank you that they are my Marys and Elizabeths in many ways—both in encouraging and in coming (to Brisbane to visit). Lord I just pray that each of us will be able to open our hearts more and more to those people around us—that we can be real, live life together. And in that way be built up to shine our lights stronger for you to those around us. In your name we pray. Amen.

BJ understood the power of encouragement. She knew how desperately she needed to be encouraged through her journey. But she also knew how much those around her needed to be encouraged. What did she really look for in a church community the most? It was the ministry of encouragement. One of the key elements of her small group gatherings was encouragement.

BJ captured the essence of a biblical method of discipling that is holistic. The encouragement is not just a "word thing." It is a "journeying thing" where people gather to journey together and share each other's load. Beagles says:

> The communal, familial nature of the church requires that its members be involved in discipling one another in everyday life, such as "when you sit in your house and when you walk by the way and when you lie down and when you rise up" (Deut 6:9 NASB). This is a far different picture from the common understanding of Christians as consumers of religious goods and services.
>
> At present there seems to be few, if any, attempts within local churches to intentionally disciple/equip adolescents within a relational, non-programmatic structure. What might local church congregations do to intentionally come alongside adolescent disciples in order to encourage, equip, and challenge them in love to grow toward maturity in Christ? It appears that it is time for the local Christian church congregation, with or without the guidance of an active youth or family ministry, to accept the role each member plays as part of an authoritative community and therefore

a vital part of what can help most to solve the crisis, as Christians view it, of the low estate of discipleship and the corollary rejection of the church by its young people.[15]

Jesus' commission to His disciples was:

> Go and make disciples of all nations, baptising them in the name of the Father and of the Son and of the Holy Spirit, and teaching them to obey everything I have commanded you. (Matt 28:19 & 20 NIV)

Traditionally the emphasis has been on the verb "go" as we hear the appeal to move into the entire world with the good news of the gospel. However, the main verb of this commission is "make disciples." The word translated "go" is actually best translated "when you have gone" or "going," "in your going." Clearly, we cannot make disciples without first going, but there is an assumption of "going." The translation could just as easily be "while you are going . . ." or "in your going . . ." make disciples. Whether we are an educator, or a labourer in a factory, or a stay-at-home mum, or a student at school . . . while we do what we do, we are commanded by Christ to make disciples.

> BJ's example is forever with me and I would love to be a fraction of what she was. I learned to put people first; to leave an open door; to be patient with people's shortcomings; to love with time and actions; to go with the flow in a different culture; to put my personal space and belongings second to people; to always be willing to get into people's lives even when they are not the primary people I am there to serve; to serve Jesus with a self-sacrificing attitude; to encourage others to do the same.[16]

BJ "invited" entrance into the discipleship experience that was a feature of her ministry. "Doing life together" was her slogan. "Walking slowly with people" was her way. It was concrete experiences of life that BJ used as points of reflection to lead others in the group into a process of meaning making, and experimentation toward life transformation. The reflection was done as a group, sharing feelings, thoughts and frustrations in an ever-deepening and transparent way. It always appeared relevant to a particular

---

15. Kathleen Beagles, "Growing Disciples in Community," *Christian Education Journal*, ser. 3, 9 (2012) 149, 156. See also Dallas Willard, *The Great Omission: Reclaiming Jesus' Essential Teachings on Discipleship* (San Francisco: HarperSanFrancisco, 2006), and Bill Hull, *The Disciple Making Pastor* (Grand Rapids: Revell, 1988).

16. Carol Dizon, e-mail message to author, May 2, 2013.

member of the group. However, the agenda was not always the experience of a member of the group that sparked the reflection. Often it was something that emerged from the passage of Scripture that the group were studying at the time. Their effort to apply the Scripture appeared to prompt connections with concrete experiences, which were then reflected upon. BJ was never into theoretical discussions or reflections on a theological truth for the sake of discovery or conversation. The reflections had to do with the "stuff" of life and had application to living authentically. She wanted to be "real" and did not want to hide behind some theoretical perspective.

While BJ's discipleship group usually met weekly, there were times when individual members were not present for a week or two at a time. There was no set programme as such, and there were numerous interactions amongst the group members between sessions. Most sessions involved sharing together that used a printed study guide as a focus. For example, they used study books from such authors as Max Lucado that were life-centred but biblically based. There was extensive sharing and prayer time together, and usually food snacks. The weekly sessions typically lasted two hours. The venue for the sessions was rotated around various members' homes, based on individual and family needs, rather than a roster system. The informality of the organisation and the timing appeared to be a strength of the group.

> Informal education (being) is the natural socialization process that takes place through human interaction in families, schools, churches, and societies. Learning takes place primarily through interaction with the social context.
>
> Non-formal education (doing) includes deliberate teaching and learning, not casual or merely circumstantial, not linked too tightly to the formal social ladder of schooling. Non-formal learning generally includes greater flexibility and freedom using experiential learning methods.[17]

Using this definition, BJ's discipleship groups were both non-formal and informal, although I suspect beyond the intentionality to meet, few of the participants would have recognised the non-formality of the learning experience. Learning appeared to take place through the serendipitous moments of sharing together.

---

17. Dean G. Blevins and Mark A. Maddix, *Discovering Discipleship: Dynamics of Christian Education* (Kansas City: Beacon Hill, 2010), 156.

Doing Life

In Brisbane, the involvement of the immediate families of the young ladies also provided for a broader curriculum from what would ordinarily have been expected. There was an air of wholesomeness and celebration as families got together. The children played together and the adults socialised in relaxed and very informal ways. Through it all there was never any sense of "this is something that I have to do." Rather it was more "this is one of the fun things we do." There is no mistaking the fact that each member had a strong relational connection with the other members, although it appeared that BJ was the "glue" for the group.

> Our little group was great to be a part of and the memories I hold from our time together, especially the time with Belinda, I will hold very close. What I liked about our group was that it was relaxed and informative without making me feel like the "bible kindergartener" that I was. Belinda had a way of explaining sections of the bible in my terms, relating it to everyday life. I always felt like an important part of the group and felt I could add to the conversations, which I had never experienced in a bible study group before.
>
> Our group focused a lot on the amazing women in the bible. Being a group of mothers, daughters, sisters and friends it was quite easy to discuss issues arising in our own lives and how to deal with them in God's way.
>
> The meetings with the girls were a great way to regularly reflect on one's life, goals and values. It was a regular reality check and kept me grounded and really thinking about what is important to me and those in my life that are of value and importance. Belinda always wrote down what we wanted to pray for, and what we gave thanks for, that week. Towards the end of BJ's battle we went over all of our prayers and how far we had all come! This was quite amazing.
>
> Another defining moment in our group was during our last time as a group together. Most meetings everyone was very reluctant to speak up and pray for the group, everyone except BJ of course! But on our trip to "the Penthouse," Belinda put it to us that we all pray for another person in the room (out loud) and tell a little of our journey towards becoming a Christian. These prayers were very deep and many tears were shed. It was very heartfelt to hear another person feel and care so much for another family/person and we could all really see how important each of us really were to each other. It was also comforting to know that everyone's

journey was not as easy or straight forward as originally thought! It was a very REAL moment.

It is very sad that our group has come to an end . . . but I think all of us know that it was never going to be the same without the driving force, the one that quietly opened our eyes to a life of Christianity . . . BJ.[18]

---

18. Melissa McCray, Facebook message to author, Apr 8, 2013.

Chapter 5

The Medical Journey

I CAN ONLY IMAGINE the whirlwind of thoughts and emotions that BJ experienced as she was thrust into a medical system that worked quickly as soon as she presented with abnormal blood test results. I know that Jacque and I were left with our minds in a whirl as we struggled to come to terms with this new reality. The first I heard of the possibility of cancer as a diagnosis was from a brief conversation with BJ by phone on October 23, 2009, while she was in Perth completing speaking engagements and undergoing medical tests. Jacque was at work and I phoned her to tell her the news. I remember meeting Jacque in the driveway of our home as she returned home from work early, falling into each other's arms and crying together. I don't think I have ever felt as anguished in spirit or as devastated as I was at that moment. The fact that we could not be with BJ through those critical days while she was still in Perth, and we in Brisbane, meant she was facing this without family around her. This made it all the more painful for us. We wanted to be there; to support her; to walk with her through these dark days. How thankful we were, though, for a church in Perth that surrounded her with love and support.[1] It was members in the church some five thousand kilometres from our home that took her to several different doctors' appointments and medical tests so that when she arrived home a lot of the diagnostics were ready for review by specialists.

There were many decisions to be made, medical procedures to be carried out, and monitoring protocols to be established. The battery of tests locating the exact type and source of the suspected cancer were in themselves traumatic. Once BJ was back in Brisbane, several more tests were conducted. There was frustration at having to go through a series of tests that slowly eliminated possibilities. I know I wanted results of tests to be

---

1. Catharine Castlehow and her family hosted BJ in Perth through these difficult days, giving of themselves sacrificially. Their church congregation at the Dianella Church of the Nazarene were equally supportive.

instant, but I had to get used to waiting several days sometimes, for results that would suggest the next step in BJ's diagnosis and subsequent treatment. It was during this time that physical symptoms became acute for BJ. Whether it was the emotions catching up with her after handling so much on her own while in Perth, or simply her condition that began to express itself in what was previously almost symptomless, I am not sure. All we know is that periods of pain wracked her body. It took high-level analgesics to bring it under control. We witnessed our bright, bubbly daughter reduced to a distraught, fatigued, and quiet young lady, often lying in a foetal position weeping quietly because of the pain. Thankfully doctors worked quickly on pain management, and although BJ learned to live with a level of constant pain, it did become manageable. Those who met her casually through the years of cancer treatment would hardly know that she lived with pain almost constantly. She learned to read the signs in her own body and became quite the master at managing it. Once the pain was under control BJ became her bright, bubbly self again.

The first medical procedure to be done was the insertion of a stent into the bowel around the site of the primary tumour. This was to ensure that the bowel remained open should the tumour continue to grow while chemotherapy was begun. As a family we often laughed together about our mealtime conversation. It would sometimes go like this:

Family: BJ, Have you had a bowel movement today?

BJ: Last night but not today.

Family: How was it? . . .

You get the picture . . . descriptions of bowel motions, etc., would lead to a discussion about appropriate medication and fluid intake to ensure a healthy bowel motion. When bowel motions normalised there was cause for celebration. I guess this wasn't normal table conversation for most families, but we all felt part of this journey through such talk. The doctors also urged the rest of the family to have colonoscopies as well, just in case BJ's cancer contained a hereditary link. BJ "sweetly" saw this as the family's identification with her and her journey! "How special!" she would say with a cheeky grin on her face!

Once the stent in the bowel was successfully in place, it was then time to visit the oncologist about chemotherapy options. A few days later BJ was in hospital again for the placement of a PICC (peripherally inserted central catheter) line into her right upper arm. So many needles! So many things to have done before treatment could start! At least it felt like progress after the intensive weeks of tests, waiting for results, and discussion.

Once the decision had been made to go down the chemotherapy route, a routine was established and BJ developed meaningful relationships with medical staff. The oncology unit staff of the Mater Public Hospital was caring, positive and engaging. Over the two years of treatment, BJ became a familiar sight on Ward 10B. Her cheerful smile and chatty disposition always inspired those around her. Occasionally she would strike up a conversation with a newly diagnosed patient and encourage them in their journey. She would allay their fears and nervousness. It was quite humorous to listen to her encourage someone, knowing that BJ herself had a "thing" about needles and injections. She became quite the expert at having numerous needles, blood samples taken, etc. BJ developed an increased pain threshold, and the ability to accept the numerous injections, many times through the gentle encouragement of the medical staff. Her stock direction to medical staff was, "Keep the medication [designed to deal with the side effects of the chemotherapy] to a minimum. I have too much I want to do this week to be lying in bed sleeping all day."

One of the first nurses that BJ met in the day oncology ward was also an acupuncturist. He was conducting research on the use of acupuncture during chemotherapy treatment. It is thought that when acupuncture is applied during treatment that it assists in the alleviation of nausea and other difficult side effects. BJ was offered the treatment. Surprising us all, she decided to go ahead and have several treatments. Her only request was that she didn't see the needles in her body! The nurse had a great sense of humour and made the experience an interesting (and almost enjoyable!) one for her, even in the midst of her anxiety at being pricked with more needles. BJ was never sure whether the treatment helped or not, but she did have acupuncture treatment each time that this particular nurse was on duty.

BJ was known as a "public" patient in the Australian health care system since she did not have private health insurance. This means she had to rely upon the socialised medical facilities in Australia for all her medical needs. Working overseas as long as she did made private health insurance impractical, particularly having to rely on donations from Australia to make ends meet. However, BJ had no complaints about the quality of care she received. It was exceptional. It was no surprise, though, that partway through her treatment she had a change of oncologists due to hospital staff changes. She needed to establish a relationship with her new oncologist who happened to be Burmese. There was an instant connection. I don't think that BJ received preferential treatment over any other public patient, but she did enjoy the benefits of an oncologist who worked hard on her behalf and who appeared to like spending time with her. On occasion, the treatment protocols were such that the government would no longer fund a very expensive drug that the oncologist believed was in BJ's best interest. The oncologist would negotiate with drug companies to have them subsidise the medication, and to our knowledge BJ never lacked the appropriate medication due to a lack of funding.

> Thank you God for a great supportive medical team!! Went to see my doctor (to check to see if I should even go to NZ) . . . and she had already told day oncology to page her as soon as I arrived—but I didn't make it there first—but nice that she was making the effort to see me. She took me into her office. I was an extra appointment and apologetic about having to see her. But she said No. She had finished with clinic patients and had time for me. She actually knew a lot on Tuesday (*previously*) but didn't want to tell me before my trip. She said she wasn't trying to keep secrets and would discuss whatever I wanted—just didn't want to spoil my holiday. She is so lovely. First is . . . my cancer is progressing. We discussed plans etc. So nice to hear she is already on to it—she is on my side and doing all she can—even called the liver surgeon and she will meet with him while I am on holidays. Just going the extra mile! Nice!
>
> Then saw Gayle (nurse from oncology) and she was lovely as we walked over to oncology together. All the nurses are wishing me well on my trip etc. and are so lovely. Mitch even commented—you have a lot of friends here haha! Even though this is a major setback and disappointing, I feel my medical team is supportive and have my best interest at heart. They are travelling this journey with me too. It makes it easier and may they see God through me. We've been on this journey over 14 months now.[2]

BJ's first chemo treatment was November 19, 2009, and initially it was scheduled every two weeks. Before chemo was given each time, a blood test was taken. BJ would then see the specialist to be given the all clear to have chemo that day. When her treatment regimen changed at one point she needed to wait at least two hours for the chemo to be prepared for

---

2. BJ diary, Jan 6, 2011.

administration. It was during these two hours that BJ was usually feeling well enough to take off to the shops or the chocolate store (Max Brenner's) for some fun with whoever was her companion for that day (most times Jacque, but many times one of her friends or another family member).

The chemo administered intravenously in the hospital would take at least three hours and then she would return home. The chemo administration was not over then, for she would have a small bottle to hang around her neck for the next forty-eight hours that slowly delivered its contents into her system. Two days later she was back to the hospital to have that drug bottle removed and the PICC line flushed out. Once home from the initial chemo administration, she would be in a drug haze. Her eyes would appear glassy and she would have difficulty focussing. She was usually unable to sleep for the next twenty-four hours because of the drugs administered along with the chemo to counter some of the nasty side-effects of the chemotherapy. Initially this was difficult for BJ, but she soon developed a rhythm where she would spend the long night hours chatting on Skype to friends in Thailand, the United States, or other parts of the world. Fortunately her friends were "night-owls" as well and Thailand time was three hours behind Brisbane time. BJ was able to maintain her fluency in the Thai language, and keep a direct contact with close friends.

On the alternate week from a hospital visit, a "Blue Care" nurse came to the house to clean the PICC line to prevent infection. Once again, BJ was able to establish a beautiful relationship with at least one of these nurses. Chats about life, where BJ found her optimistic and hope-filled attitude, and what the latest activity that BJ was involved in, all became topics of conversation with these nurses who were quite used to dealing with sorrow and heartache. When we ultimately needed a nurse to verify that BJ had died at home and fill out the appropriate paper work, one of the Blue Care nurses, now working other cases, asked to do the task. This was more than a job to her. Once she had completed the task of verification, I left her alone with BJ to grieve and reflect. Tears were shed and thoughts were shared that were much more than a nurse simply doing her job. We were humbled and touched at the respectful way this was handled.

BJ was initially diagnosed as having 4th-stage bowel cancer with secondary cancers in the liver and lung. Of greatest concern was the liver. Initially, the chemo worked well and the hope was that enough of the cancer would clear from the liver so that the diseased portion of the liver could be removed by surgery. Once that was done then surgery would be conducted to take care of the bowel and lungs. This was going to be a difficult and complex journey, but we had a focus for our prayers, and pray we did. So many people around the world prayed! Unfortunately while the cancer count in the blood tests dropped dramatically the liver was still covered with lesions. Our prayers were not being answered in the way we had hoped.

To have the initial good response to the chemo turn to bad news (that the liver remained covered with lesions) came as a real disappointment. BJ had already made major decisions about how she would approach life. However the relentless attack on her body by both the cancer and the chemotherapy, and what now appeared to be a longer term process, produced times of discouragement. Bright and sparkling, BJ may have been; she was also committed to being authentic. Learning to live with "chemo-brain" as she called it, was a frustration for her. She described it as "living in a fog." Slowness in response, and waves of incredible tiredness frustrated her. She wanted to do more, go to more places, and engage more. Her focus shifted from looking to tomorrow, to surviving the challenges of today. There were bad days of feeling terrible and living with some pain. She learned to endure those, and when good days came, she lived them for all she was worth! We prayed as a family, we lived our schedules around what needed to be done medically for BJ, and we agonised over the discouragements.

> Chemo day—all went well and quickly. A good thing ☺. PICC line bled quickly and well!! But bad blood tests results ☹. CEA is way up over 700 so this was very disappointing. I feel disappointed, discouraged and scared . . . but I hold onto hope! I am so grateful for my faith in an unchanging, ever-giving, ever faithful God!! It's all I have! Oh, and my amazing support network.[3]

One of the constant dangers that BJ lived with was that of infection. She had decided that she was not going to seclude herself to avoid the risk of infection. We did everything possible as a family to minimise the risk, however. Anyone coming to our home had the routine of hand washing with antiseptic lotion, and anyone with a cold or flu was discouraged from visiting. However, we could not minimise infection risk when BJ attended functions with large groups such as football games, concerts, or general church life. So, the inevitable would happen from time to time. Once BJ's body temperature reached 38 degrees Celsius it was off to the emergency room at the hospital. Despite having all the documentation outlining her

3. BJ diary, Jan 4, 2011.

The Medical Journey

condition and the treatment protocols that were needed, we soon learned that the best place to take her was to the hospital where she was receiving treatment, about a forty-minute drive from home. Nevertheless, each time I took her to the emergency room it meant I would be there for several hours. The spikes in body temperature always seemed to happen very late at night or the small hours of the morning. This usually meant a night of no sleep for both of us! These times in the hospital were very difficult times for BJ, not because of challenging treatment plans, but because of frustration at having to change plans she had made to be elsewhere. It was more difficult for friends to visit the hospital than home, and she was usually isolated in a room for fear of further infection. There were sound medical reasons for all of this but she bored easily.

The Australian health system worked well in care of BJ with her terminal illness. Sometimes a social worker would call in at the hospital to see what kind of support BJ may need. Each time she came to visit, the social worker would see somebody different sitting with BJ through her chemo session. On a number of occasions she would ask, "How many people do you have around you BJ? I don't think you need any support from me. You appear to have so much." BJ's response was always with a smile, "O yes, I have plenty, thanks for asking!" Then rather facetiously she would add, "I have worked up a roster so everyone gets a turn at bringing me to chemo!" In our home the "roster" was called the "chemo run" for the chemo treatment and the "bottle run" for the time she had to go back to the hospital for about thirty minutes to have the chemo bottle removed forty-eight hours after treatment. If a family member couldn't do the "run," then there were always plenty of friends willing to do so.

Once it was apparent that BJ was handling the chemotherapy relatively well, it was suggested that she have a "portacath" put in to replace the PICC line. BJ resisted this suggestion because it meant another day surgery appointment and "more needles!" Eventually the PICC line did get infected but because of the difficult timing, the doctors replaced her PICC line in her right arm with one in her left arm. The process went smoothly but the doctors continued to recommend the portacath. Eventually the timing was right, and BJ finally consented to the insertion of the portacath, placed under the skin just a few inches below the shoulder; another trip to the hospital and another day of learning new things. However, the procedure went smoothly, and BJ soon had greater flexibility showering, etc., for the first time in over eighteen months. The one down side to having the porta-cath was that she did not need to have it flushed every week. That meant no visit by the Blue Care nurses. BJ had to find other ways to keep connected, which, being BJ, she did. The occasional morning tea with "her special nurse" did the trick.

> Felicity, the Blue Care nurse came to visit—how lovely! Again the genuine concern of nurses is so nice.[4]

> Good morning tea with Felicity, my Blue Care nurse. It's nice how much they care and visit even though she is not nursing me now.[5]

The day oncology unit at the Mater Public Hospital became a very familiar place. Those working there came to know BJ and one or two developed a good relationship with her. One of the nurses literally bumped into BJ when she was completing a 10km "Bridge to Brisbane" walk as a fund-raiser for cancer research. The nurse was amazed and thrilled that BJ was involved. BJ was walking with a couple of her discipleship girls and raised substantial funds for cancer research. She completed the walk! Proudly displayed in the oncology unit at the hospital is a photo of Belinda and the nurse participating in the "Bridge to Brisbane" walk. From then on, the nurse continued to Facebook with Belinda and follow her journey—a connection that Jacque has now continued.

> Thank you God for the Mater Hospital. It really has become a second home—the nurses all know me, and I feel part of the furniture haha!! Gayle (nurse) is a FB friend . . . and she saw my Ps 13 status and was very concerned with what it was about. That's so nice . . . her concern. It is so cool that my status led her to find a Bible verse (she doesn't normally read the Bible she told me). Lord, even in my down days . . . use me![6]

Occasionally the nursing staff would ask BJ to talk with a patient who was having a particularly bad time adjusting to their own diagnosis, or was apprehensive about a procedure that BJ had already gone through. It seemed that they saw in BJ someone who brought strength, hope and optimism to

---

4. BJ diary, June 17, 2011.
5. Ibid., Dec 15, 2011.
6. Ibid., June 16, 2011.

The Medical Journey

the ward. BJ did not see herself as medically inclined at all. One of her greatest challenges as a missionary in Thailand was taking children to the emergency room at the local hospital for treatment of broken limbs or bad gashes. Blood, needles and all things medical made her shudder at best and sometimes faint. But here she was, talking patients through a medical procedure from her own experience and alleviating fears. Remarkable!

> Bad scan results and a CEA reading (995)—shows growth on my liver. But I praise God for being able to handle hearing these results. I also praise God that funding is available to continue with my drugs even though I am a "progressing patient." I praise God for how far I have come, fear and pain wise—telling people a PICC doesn't hurt to come out etc., having acupuncture (and this was just today). I thank Him for giving me strength for this day and taking away fear.[7]

> Met a girl (a lady ☺) at chemo (bottle off) today—same cancer but just starting her journey and her liver seems a lot better than mine—the marks are on one side—nice!! But it was so nice to meet someone else, similar age, female, with the same cancer! What a blessing. Thanx God![8]

This young lady did respond well to the chemo and was able to have the surgery that BJ had so hoped for herself. BJ rejoiced at the news of good progress for this young lady, despite her own disappointing medical results.

By early 2011 it was apparent that the treatment regime was not bringing any improvement, even though it appeared to be holding the cancer at bay. The troubling question that arose was, "Is there more we can do? What about alternative treatment plans?" I was pleasantly surprised at the open response I received from the oncologist as I verbalised these questions. She was by no means closed to the idea of a fresh approach. The doctor went on to explain that she had taken BJ's case to a conference for discussion to see whether others may have other ideas of treatment plans. The oncologist was aware that her professional liaisons were in a relatively small circle. To think creatively perhaps it required someone from outside her usual group of consultants to give insight. Unfortunately, the conference did not bring any further insight or suggestions for different directions in treatment. In the light of this, the oncologist did offer to facilitate a second opinion. This

---

7. Ibid., Jan 20, 2011.
8. Ibid., Sept 7, 2011.

would mean a trip to Melbourne or Adelaide to reach into a different community of oncologists. A trip to one or both of these cities was seriously considered, but each time we thought of trying, BJ's condition required more direct care—an infection, an adverse blood test result—or there appeared to be an indication that the current treatment was beginning to have the desired effect. We settled to having discussions with BJ's oncologist and her accounts of conversations with oncologists outside of her normal consultative circle. BJ's oncologist did set up an appointment with a specialist in another leading hospital in Brisbane to explore the possibility of placing radioactive rods directly into the tumours of the liver. While this was a possibility, it appeared that BJ's condition did not quite meet the necessary protocols in a number of the alternative approaches.

The conversations about her medical journey were not restricted to medical staff.

> Awesome chats! So many lately about my cancer and why I think bad things happen to Christians, and how I cope etc. This morning in English class it was just Joseph so we had a D & M (deep and meaningful) for 40 minutes. I think I made him cry (in a good way). Then lunch with Carine and Mel (Carine's bridesmaid)—the chance to talk about it again. Crazy! I really see God in all of these chats—people want to know—I thank God He has given me things to say, a confidence in Him, and a peace about the situation. I have also grown from all of these chats. I thank God for friends with real concern.[9]

The oncology unit tended to attract nurses from all over the world, and this was something that BJ enjoyed immensely. Medical staff came from Vietnam, Scotland, England, New Zealand, Burma, Russia, Thailand, Philippines. . . . One nurse, originally from Vietnam, but one who had worked in Europe as well, continued as a Facebook friend with BJ and now with Jacque. This multicultural setting was a very pleasant place for BJ. She enjoyed the interactions of so many, the cultural nuances, and the shared stories. She felt right at home. Another of the nurses was a Christian who enjoyed times chatting with BJ about her faith. This nurse was thrilled that BJ had such a radiant testimony. This nurse was able to have significant faith conversations with other staff members as a result of BJ's testimony. Only eternity will tell the full extent of BJ's impact for the kingdom of God as a

---

9. Ibid., Mar 31, 2011.

The Medical Journey

result of a faithful, enthusiastic and hope-filled walk with Jesus amongst these people.

Of course the medical journey was one that did not go well a lot of the time. Looking back we see that the chemo gave BJ an extra two and a half years of life, but the prognosis was always going to be bad news, but for the grace of God. The following excerpts from BJ's "Thank You" diary give an indication of the highs and lows of her medical journey.

> Got to have chemo today. Yeah!! . . . since last week I missed it. Can't afford to miss anymore. Who would have ever thought I would say "yeah" about having chemo. Oh how my life is now so different.[10]
>
> All I can say today is thank you God for getting me through this day! Feel sick, tired, and major chemo-head in class today . . . but He got me through.[11]
>
> I thank God for one needle!! Had to have a scan today—because of my sore shoulder . . . I was worried about how long (and how many needles) it would take until they found a vein that worked . . . sent out texts to praying friends . . . and it was just one needle!! What an answer to prayer![12]
>
> Good news! My neck scan came back clear! And I am K. Ras type cancer—which means I can take the new drug! Yeah!! Thanks God for some good news—I really needed that now!![13]
>
> In hospital, but finally in the ward after 13 hours in emergency. I thank God for my own room. I thank God that I don't feel too bad. I thank God for great friends visiting tonight—Mel and Kaz came, and great friends calling and texting etc.[14]
>
> No chemo today—kinda a sad thing . . . but starting the new drug next week—so that should be good. Scary . . . but good! Hopefully

---

10. Ibid., Feb 24, 2011.
11. Ibid., Feb 28, 2011.
12. Ibid., Mar 3, 2011.
13. Ibid., Mar 24, 2011.
14. Ibid., Apr 12, 2011.

it will do something!! And it should mean I have more energy for the next week ☺.[15]

Chemo day! I'm not sure it's a good thing, but I'm glad for less drugs and less side effects. It makes the day easier even though it is given every week.[16]

Chemo day. It's been nice just hanging with Mum. Now we have two hours to wait for the drug. We've been doing different things—into the city, walk to Southbank. Nice—relaxing! Thanks Mum for taking me to chemo every Thursday—your day off!! What sacrifice! I love you.[17]

My rash. I do thank God for my rash—even though I feel ugly—I know it means my drugs are working—with the pains etc. I have at the moment I need to cling to that.[18]

Finally finding a vein (4 attempts). Thank you God that I am much better at having needles. Scan today.[19]

Scan results were good!! I am still finding it hard to fully believe!! Mum and Dad didn't go on their holiday yet because they wanted to be with me when I got the results. We were all expecting bad results. The doctor came in and said, "Good news! The tumours are shrinking!" That's pretty much all she said. I couldn't believe it!! Came home and put as my status in FB and within hours hundreds of comments and "likes." Thank you Lord!! I don't know how much shrinkage is happening, but it is!! So good to have some positive news at long last!![20]

Back to the previous chemo—but wow! Already pains have left and I have energy—granted it may be the steroids—but hey, I'll take that!! It's so nice to have energy again!! I was feeling so gross

---

15. Ibid., Apr 17, 2011.
16. Ibid., Apr 28, 2011.
17. Ibid., May 12, 2011.
18. Ibid., June 21, 2011.
19. Ibid., June 27, 2011.
20. Ibid., June 30, 2011.

The Medical Journey

when I went into chemo—I was really worried about going back on to this chemo—but so far so good. Thanks God!![21]

Chemo day and bad news. Cancer count has gone through the roof. I'm still trying to remain positive and I thank God for placing that Spirit in me because it is really hard!![22]

A very hard day! Not allowed to have chemo and not allowed to go to Manila ☹☹☹. Sent for scan. Despite of this horrible day I thank God for my amazing support. People who really care! People who know my disappointment about Manila and text me. Spent most of the day crying, but again, with friends. Thank you Lord I am not doing it alone. Thank you Lord for only 8 needles at the liver scan ☺.[23]

My belly is a pregnant belly—looks like at least 9 months! It's so ugly and has been so painful. I'm over it and want it gone. Had I litre of fluids taken out of it today—so maybe dropped to six months. Still so ugly and gross. It worries me—I don't want this anymore. But no fever today! No fever for over 24 hours!! Yeah! Thank you God![24]

Got to have chemo today even if it did take all day to have it, then home! So nice to be home! Hopefully this belly will begin to go down.[25]

A normal chemo day! It's so nice to have one of those again ☺. And the approval to go to Thailand—Yeah!! The nurses and doctors were all so lovely today—in the morning it was like all the nurses were so happy to see me—so sweet. It really has become a second home.[26]

I got to have chemo! I was really expecting (since I had been sick on the weekend) that something would be wrong and I couldn't

---

21. Ibid., Aug 22, 2011.
22. Ibid., Sept 19, 2011.
23. Ibid., Oct 17, 2011.
24. Ibid., Nov 21, 2011.
25. Ibid., Nov 22, 2011.
26. Ibid., Dec 5, 2011.

> ... but I could! Yeah! Still on track (for Thailand). Thanks God for not having to stay overnight in hospital![27]
>
> All clear from the doctor (to visit Thailand)! Love a good doctor's visit ☺!! Good hang time with Mum and Dad.[28]
>
> A normal chemo day! I feel it has been ages since I've had that!! ☺!! ... and I just took my temperature—it was 36.5—normal!! The last week it has been sitting in the 37s. So glad it is down again[29].

Despite the overall decline in BJ's health she was able to make her trip to Thailand December 29, 2011. After a couple of days in Bangkok, however, there was a significant deterioration in her condition.

> An extremely difficult day!! Plenty of tears, hurts, pains etc. ... ended with going into hospital Jan 1. But I am thankful to God for Simon who spent New Year's Eve just sitting listening to me cry and complain etc. I just lie on the floor fighting off fevers and he had to get everything for me. A true friend. We got 7/11 snacks and had our own New Year Eve party and prayed together when New Year hit. Good to have a friend who just understands.[30]

It was very important that BJ make this trip for a number of reasons, despite the risks and the likelihood that it would be cut short. First, the occasion that had her in Thailand was the 3rd Wave Global Youth Leadership Conference for the Church of the Nazarene. This was the conference that several years previously, BJ had agreed to coordinate in Bangkok. She was the logical choice as coordinator: she spoke Thai, had great connections with people in Bangkok, and had the respect of many of the Nazarene young people in the Southeast Asia Field who would be needed to assist in putting this conference together. It attracted young people from all around the world and attracts the "cream" of the Nazarene youth internationally.

The conference planning was fraught with difficulty right from the beginning. The conference site was flooded out several months prior to the event, which led to the decision to postpone the conference for twelve months. Because of the enormous damage to the original site, a new site had to be found. This was one of the tasks BJ had before returning to Brisbane

27. Ibid., Dec 12, 2011.
28. Ibid., Dec 16, 2011.
29. Ibid., Dec 19, 2011.
30. Ibid., Dec 31, 2011.

on home assignment in September 2009. The whole time BJ was in Brisbane living through the cancer experience, she was spending a significant amount of time talking with Thai contacts and coaching Peter and Leanne Clarke through the coordination process. Peter and Leanne were volunteer ministry colleagues with BJ the last twelve months she lived in Thailand. They graciously agreed to come back for another twelve months to pick up the slack created by BJ's absence. The conference gave BJ a goal—she so wanted to at least attend the conference to see all this come together after so much turmoil, both organisationally and personally.

BJ was given clearance to travel and this was a dream come true for her. She arrived a few days prior to the conference so she could see a few of her Thai friends and enjoy time with ministry colleagues. The day before the official opening of the conference, all the Asia Pacific youth attendees gathered. She knew the vast majority of these young people personally, and it was special for her to spend time with them. They had prayed for her, made regular contact with her, and many were dear friends. This was another important reason to make the trip, for it brought closure to a special chapter in her life.

> Thank you God that I could catch up with everyone!! Especially all the Asia Pacific peeps!! So fun. So great! Everyone is so super encouraging!! Just awesome to be a part of this.[31]

> Huge day! Started by going to hospital again—they wanted to admit me—so much money!!—but thank you God they understood. Even gave me lots of meds! Thank God that I got to see the girls that came down from Maetang as soon as I got out of the taxi (Kip, Sunee and Susu). So special!! Kip and I cried and cried! The day was just spent in my room (like a hospital) with visitors all day—mainly from Chiang Mai—like family. But had to make the decision to go home ☹. But I thank God that I got on the midnight flight so I had plenty of time to say goodbye to everyone. I feel it was a good closure. And I do thank God for such caring leaders who kinda made it all happen— yet included me in on the decision. I know they really care and love me—again like family. Lord, I thank God for my Christian family!! It really has been my encouragement and kept me going these past two years. I thank God for our answered prayer of getting Natalie (Ward) a visa for Australia to travel home with me. I thank God for the support all the way to the airport. Another blessed time! Family! I thank God

31. Ibid., Jan 2, 2012.

for getting me on the flight even though I was feeling so sick! I felt peace—it was the right choice![32]

I thank God for a safe flight and that I made it!! I thank God for the wheelchair service to get through the Brisbane airport—all the way to Mum! I thank God for friendly and helpful doctors and nurses and being admitted into hospital (I mean that was why I came home) . . . and I really thank God for a private room!!! So nice!! So much easier to have visitors, to do things, to have the TV on without having to wear earphones, to talk on the phone etc. etc.[33] (Jan 4, 2012).

BJ alludes to the support she received in getting her home to Brisbane. It was totally awesome! I want to acknowledge the amazing work that Verne Ward, then Asia Pacific regional director for the Church of the Nazarene, and his wife, Natalie, did to facilitate this. They phoned me several times back in Australia to describe BJ's deteriorating physical condition and to seek advice on what BJ should do. It was obvious that she needed to return home as soon as possible. Our fear was that her health would deteriorate to such a state that she would not be able to fly home. However, convincing BJ of that fact in a way that was affirming and met her needs was the challenge. From BJ's own diary, it can be seen that Verne and Natalie succeeded admirably!

As preparations were made to get a flight home, BJ tearfully said that she would so like to say farewell to people "properly." Her close Thai friends had been ministering to her in her hotel room, and this was good from the standpoint that they could see how sick she really was. Publicly BJ did a great job at not showing the physical challenges that she faced every day of her journey through cancer. Many people did not realise that she was as sick as she was. Verne Ward asked a key question of BJ as preparations were made to get her home. "What would a 'proper' farewell look like, BJ?" Her immediate response was, "A time of sharing in worship!" That simple response speaks volumes as to BJ's orientation to life and service. Her "God time" with friends was a part of who she was. Time alone with God was great, but made even richer when shared with friends. Her life was an act of worship and I cannot read Romans 12:1 without thinking of BJ's response to this question.

32. Ibid., Jan 3, 2012.
33. Ibid., Jan 4, 2012.

> I appeal to you therefore, brothers and sisters, by the mercies of God, to present your bodies as a living sacrifice, holy and acceptable to God, *which is your spiritual worship.* (Rom 12:1 NRSV, emphasis mine)

The plane was not due to leave Bangkok until midnight January 3, 2012, so arrangements were made to get BJ to the opening worship service of the 3rd Wave conference, and then on to the airport. There was great singing and praising God. Partway through the service, BJ was acknowledged and many young people crowded around to give their final farewells. What a special moment for BJ. One of her deepest desires—to worship with Nazarene youth from around the world—had been met. Thank you, 3rd Wavers, for making this possible!

The "silent" partner in all of this was Natalie Ward. She chose to accompany BJ back to Brisbane and took time out of her demanding schedule to do just that. It meant organising a visa, organising travel documents for herself, but all this was done with grace, speed and sensitivity. It was Natalie that organised the wheel chair; it was Natalie that helped BJ look smart enough to get on the plane after being bedridden for a day or so previously. There was always the risk that the airlines would refuse to take BJ because of the serious nature of her illness. It was Natalie that carried all the bags (BJ never travelled lightly!). What an amazing church to have such caring take precedence over a program—as important as that event was!

Natalie guided BJ through customs on arrival in Brisbane and was met by Jacque. They then took BJ from the Brisbane International Airport directly to the Mater Public Hospital where she was admitted immediately. When the oncologist saw BJ's condition, she was shocked at the rapid deterioration. There was no doubt that there had been a significant escalation in the growth of the cancer.

> A new pain relief drug—haven't had any pain since! And I feel more alive. Feel normal except for this massive thing—stomach and upper area.[34]

> An active day, no pain! Not feeling very sleepy. Easier to move around. ☺ Feeling better in myself. Lots of visitors. The day went fast. Started with an hour God time—devotion, prayer, write in here (the diary), worship music. Call from Derene—great conversation including tears. Visits: Mum and Grandma, Begg family,

---

34. BJ diary, Jan 6, 2012.

Dad, Grandma and Grandpa, Mitch, Muz, Bev, Kenn and Andrea. Phone call with Mel; and another phone call with Mel ☺. Watched great Louie Giglio sermon "Welcome to the story of God." Get in His story. Everything He created, including us, is to bring glory to God. May my life be all about that!![35]

Another fun day in hospital (weird to say that I know). Family (Mum, Dad, Mitch and Grandma Dudley) came in for church, which was so special! Bruce C also ended coming right as we were about to start, so he joined in too. Dad read some Scripture, we watched a great Louie Giglio sermon from Dad's "Passion 2011" DVD. It was a really good one! About making our lives count and being able to change the world despite our circumstances (including dying from cancer). About how our life sings a song and that it is our lives that "preach" at a funeral. Anyway, there was so much great stuff in it!! And then we finished with "Amazing Grace / My chains Are Gone" on a Michael W Smith DVD. Great Service!! More nice visits . . . And hospital food hasn't been that bad. LOL. Other things to thank God for: showered on my own totally—fully dressed; they found the source of the infection; no fevers; lovely nurses.[36]

Jacque and I met with one of BJ's doctors who clearly indicated that BJ was now in need of daily nursing care. It was decision time for us as a family as we saw BJ's physical life ebbing away. Should we nurse BJ at home or find a place where medical care could be more accessible? For BJ it wasn't so much medical care access, but people access, that was important. BJ was a "people person" to the very core of her being. When I am unwell I like to go away by myself, feel miserable by myself, and then reengage with people once I am feeling better. BJ was the very opposite. She was genuinely energised by having people around her. It was not a sense of insecurity, but rather a strong desire to engage with people no matter what. Soon after her first diagnosis with cancer, we had placed a mattress in the formal lounge area of our home so that she could lay there and be present in the conversations that took place when visitors arrived. She did not want to be isolated in her bedroom, no matter how sick she was. When just the family were around she would lay on the lounge in the family room so she could be a part of the normal family conversations and activities. This fact about BJ's nature helped suggest the way forward.

35. Ibid., Jan 7, 2012.
36. Ibid., Jan 8, 2012.

The Medical Journey

Jacque decided to take time off from her job at the local public school to look after BJ at home. It was easy for me to agree, but I did realise that the bulk of the caring would fall upon Jacque's shoulders. I was able to secure some time off as well that allowed me to drop by the office occasionally, rather than every day. BJ was released from hospital on January 10, 2012. Jacque became BJ's full-time carer which was much more than simply helping BJ to shower; she became social secretary; medication manager; conduit of information to a variety of church committees and small groups whose responsibilities BJ needed to release to others; hospitality coordinator; mum. Jacque's days and nights were full. Prior to this time we had organised our family (and sometimes work life) around BJ's health needs, but now her needs became the dominating issue for us all. Most nights were punctuated with times of being with BJ and we all learned to live on snatches of sleep when we could. Having said that, we would have it no other way. BJ continued to be an inspiration to all that came by to see her.

January 16, 2012, became the next major step in BJ's medical journey.

> Heard the worst news today—no more treatment—only weeks to live. In my heart I knew, but so hard to hear. But what am I thankful for today? The *amazing* support that has gotten me through this life / this day. My parents have just been pillars of strength!! I am just so amazed at how strong my Mum has been during all of this. She is holding me up (literally too LOL). I have also had many many others surround me with support as I tell people.
>
> I also thank God for the peace You have given me—yes I am sad, scared, angry etc., but more than that—I have a hope and a peace. A reminder (and this is a big one) that God is in control of each moment.
>
> I thank God for the goodbyes I got to have with the nurses that were there today (Kris, Josh, Lyn, Helen, and especially Ruth). Ruth was just so out there about her and my faith. She told me how it had touched so many nurses there. And gave me so many words of encouragement—it was super special.[37]

BJ made a tearful farewell to the day oncology staff at the Ward 10B at the Mater Public Hospital. The final chapter of BJ's illness had begun. We had all anticipated this day, but when it arrived, it was still difficult news to accept. Our first decision was to decide where BJ would spend the last days of her life—in a hospice centre or at home. From Jacque's point of

---

37. BJ diary, Jan 16, 2012.

view there was no real alternative but to nurse BJ at home. BJ was glad and grateful for this decision.

It was now time to turn to palliative care. We realised that what we saw of BJ now was the best it was going to be, and that we needed to prepare to see a further deterioration in her physical condition. This was an extremely emotionally taxing time for all of us. News was out amongst BJ's many friends about this latest event, so a steady stream of visitors were there to see BJ. As part of our commitment to care for BJ at home also meant that we would host many people in our home, anxious to say their farewells to BJ.

Rather than going out for medical appointments, now, medical personnel came to our home. The palliative care doctor and nurse came by to see BJ and to talk to us about what could be expected in the next few weeks. Jacque and I were now in problem-solving mode, as BJ was given further pain relief that made things more comfortable for her. Along with the pain relief came sluggish responses and much more sleeping. BJ's expressed intentions were clear—she did not want to be "bombed out" with medication, so it was important that minimal pain relief be given with the possibility of us managing the breakthrough pain when it occurred. This is what we tried to do over the next few weeks.

> Endone. Haha!! I thank God for the medication that helps me with the pain! I am thankful for medical help. I'm disappointed that there is really nothing that can help me now—but I know chemo has given me a good 2 years and I am so thankful for those 2 years! It has been an amazing journey. And now the meds help me stay pain free—which is nice!! It really helps me to cope! I had a lot of pain today—and crying and stuff. Wasn't fun—so endone really helped! I thank the Lord for the medical profession that has taken such good care of me. The Mater Hospital staff has become like good friends. How special. Saying goodbye to them was hard. Plenty of tears. And now Felicity—under palliative care—how lovely she is!! Just goes out of her way to help. Lord may you bless all these dear workers. May you continue to help scientists make breakthroughs in developing cures for cancer.[38]

The next step was to mobilise what resources we could to assist Jacque in the nursing care required. Mitch and I were also at home a reasonable amount of time since it was holiday season, and so we tried to make this a shared family responsibility. Even so, the bulk of the tasks fell to Jacque.

---

38. Ibid., Jan 29, 2012.

The Medical Journey

Mitch and I were available with the lifting and moving needed that eased Jacque's burden. The health care system in Australia caters well for palliative care in the home. By this time BJ's abdomen was swelling uncomfortably and mobility became an issue. Her feet had begun to swell and walking was difficult, and really contraindicated because it just exacerbated the problem.

> I thank God for my wheelchair! ☺ Thanx God for the provision of all these things. The fact we have them available at no cost is such a blessing! The wheelchair enables me to get out and about—which I *so* need. It is nice and light—easy to take places and comfortable which is all such a blessing. Also the toilet chair—*so* much easier . . . I love it! . . . I also got a monkey grip from the palliative care team. This is also nice to have to move around the bed and just a comfort to know it's there. I have stayed in bed for several nights (what a good little girl). Things like Dad putting in the TV etc. has really helped that!![39]

The palliative nurse called at home every two or three days and the doctor weekly, at least until the final few days. This was amazingly helpful as we sought to manage BJ's increasing number of symptoms. For example, when BJ became so uncomfortable with her swollen belly, the palliative care nurse facilitated the appointment for BJ to get to the hospital for draining of the tumours.

> Thank you Lord! 4.8 litres drained today!! What else can I say but I just got rid of a huge baby and hopefully I'll be able to walk some more. That is heavy to be carrying around—and I still look huge—just not as tight which is nice. Yeah! I have a belly button back. It all happened so smoothly. 15 minutes for the ultrasound and then the drain started. I found out later they had squashed me in because they saw my name. How lovely! So worth cancelling all my visitors here. And seeing the nurses again is always fun—like friends. Today has been a day of great blessings, and Lord I thank you for everything—even the small things. Sorry they are getting overlooked with all these huge blessings. Family dinner tonight was just lovely. I thank Lord for how close our family has become through all of this!! Keep it a coming Lord!! ☺[40]

Another difficult decision that we needed to face, along with BJ, was the decision whether to resuscitate or not, should BJ fall into a medical

---

39. Ibid., Jan 14, 2012.
40. Ibid., Feb 2, 2012.

crisis and an ambulance might need to be called. Documents needed to be signed so that ambulance personnel would know not to medically intervene in what was now the inevitable. I remember this conversation vividly. BJ looked at the palliative care doctor and said, "I am not afraid of dying, but I am scared about what I might experience toward the end. What can I expect? Will it be painful?" The doctor's response was beautifully reassuring. He indicated that it was his job to keep BJ free from pain and he could do that with medication. He said quite simply that as the pain increased, he would increase the level of medication so that she was pain free. It would ultimately mean that the last few hours or days of life she should be asleep. She would then pass away while sleeping. BJ's response to that was, "Oh, I can do that!"

The decision was made not to resuscitate should medical personnel be called. Papers were signed and I was left with a knot in my stomach and a deep ache in my heart. A question, "Could we have done more?" haunted me. Rationally I know that everything was done, but that didn't stop the sense of helplessness and despair engulfing me. BJ had faced these last days with incredible dignity and grace. She exuded an air of gratefulness that inspired and comforted. When I was carrying her to the bathroom for the last time, just before she was unable to toilet herself, with her arms around my neck, she whispered in my ear, "I love you, Dad. Thanks for all you are doing for me." Those words will stay with me for the rest of my life. It was all I could do to tell her that I loved her too. It appeared that she knew I was haunted by the question of "Could we have done more?" Those words assured me that all had been done that could be done, and she was content. She was ready to go.

During the last week of BJ's life we kept a twenty-four-hour vigil beside her bed. At least one of the family, and often one of the discipleship girls sat through the long nights, reading, playing her favourite songs and chatting with her when she was awake. The night of February 14, 2012 (her last night with us), Jacque and I spent the night with her. Partway through the night her breathing became laboured and noisy. The doctor had prepared us for this and said that he could further medicate her when this stage started, but that she was in no distress. The medication would be more for our benefit than hers. We decided to honour her wish to be as lightly medicated as possible, and sat through several hours of noisy breathing that signalled the

The Medical Journey

end was near. By seven o'clock BJ's breathing became irregular and at eight o'clock in the morning, February 15, 2012, BJ breathed her last breath on this earth. She had not communicated with us for over forty-eight hours, but as she was taking her last breath, she turned her head toward Jacque and Mel and smiled. That smile stayed on her face even in death.

Carine, our daughter-in-law, posted on Facebook at BJ's passing:

> Belinda, you fought a brave fight. You're a hero and an inspiration to everyone you've met. And you will continue to be. You went out with a smile on your face. Guess the view what was awaiting you is everything you imagined it to be. We miss you. We love you.[41]

> When this perishable body puts on imperishability, and this mortal body puts on immortality, then the saying that is written will be fulfilled: "Death has been swallowed up in victory. Where, O death is your victory? Where, O death, is your sting?" . . . But thanks be to God, who gives us the victory through our Lord Jesus Christ. (1 Cor 15:54–56 NRSV)

---

41. Carine Kellens Allder, "Under His Sky" Facebook page (accessed Feb 15, 2012), http://www.facebook.com/UnderHisSky.

Chapter 6

The Family Journey

When life serves up a "curve ball," or more accurately a "bouncer" in cricket parlance, all of a sudden that which is predictable in life seems to disappear. Our immediate family moved into "autopilot" as we kept doing what we needed to do in our jobs, yet trying to come to terms with the fact that BJ had been diagnosed with a terminal illness. Tim, just a couple of years younger than BJ, was quite used to relating to BJ as a peer. Carine, Tim's wife, also became an integral part of this family journey.

> An awesome arvo (afternoon) with Carine. We got to buy random things and had amazing chats—from real girly ones to everything—it's like we really are sisters now.[1]

Mitch, on the other hand, had never really related to BJ as a peer and brother until BJ returned home and was diagnosed with cancer. From the age of six, Mitch had not been around BJ much. She had travelled, worked in Sydney, London and then Thailand. To actually live in the same house and see each other almost every day allowed for a good brother/sister relationship to develop between them. In their quiet way, both Tim (and Carine) and Mitch were some of BJ's greatest supporters through the two and half years of BJ's illness. BJ's diagnosis brought us together as a family as we combined our individual strengths to assist in every way we could. My relationship with Jacque deepened. As we have faced challenging times in the past we have done so together, leaning on one another, often unsure of anything but our love for each other and our commitment to make it through together. This particular experience, perhaps more so than any other we have had to this point in our marriage, has thrust us together producing a stronger more resilient relationship with our God, with each other, and with our boys.

1. BJ diary, June 3, 2010.

The Family Journey

When it looked like BJ would lose her hair through chemo treatment, Mitch joined BJ's other friends in shaving off his long curly locks in solidarity with his sister. Tim, for the last six months of BJ's life, booked only tours that allowed him to be accessible to Brisbane so he could be available for BJ if needed. Carine was available to assist as needs arose at many inconvenient times. Family meals together took on much more significance and Christmas, birthdays and other anniversaries became a focal point. In the back of our minds we wondered whether this would be the last time we could all be together for this particular celebration. Mitch as a young adult was able to go to movies with BJ, be involved in church youth groups together, and generally relate as young adults. Mitch also took his "turn" at taking BJ to chemo treatments and being taxi when BJ was too sick to drive herself places. They both valued those times together.

> I thank you God for Mitch—had my first guitar lesson with him. Thanx for the time I've been able to spend with him! It is good to go out with Mitch to the movies ☺[2]

> I thank God for Mitch's constant help to me. We had a great hang out day shopping in the city. We never hang out so it was really nice![3]

The extended family also made it a priority to be present at family gatherings. We at least had some warning that BJ's life was to be shortened and we were able to celebrate the time we did have with her.

BJ never really grew up when it came to Christmas. When at home (from very small through to and including adulthood) she was always the first to rise on Christmas morning. This is a girl who would rarely "do mornings," and then only when she had to, any other time of the year! However, from four o'clock in the morning, BJ would be out of bed and waking the household ready for the distribution of gifts. We have a family tradition of having bacon and eggs for Christmas morning breakfast before going to church. She would begin clattering around in the kitchen if no one had responded to her wake-up calls. Christmas music would be blaring, Christmas lights on, and it was hard not to catch the enthusiasm of gift giving. BJ, like Jacque, loved to give gifts and so they always gave a small thoughtful gift to each of the extended family as a way of thanking God for family. Our last Christmas together (2011) was a gathering of both my and

2. Ibid., Oct 9, 2010.
3. Ibid., Mar 4, 2011.

Jacque's extended family. What a great time of sharing together—a large enough group that we rented the NTC Student Common Room for our celebration lunch! Lots of children, laughter, and good food marked the day as we bowed our heads at the beginning of the meal to thank God for another Christmas that we could all be together. No longer were these celebrations taken for granted. Each one was savoured and relished with grateful hearts. How much longer were we going to have her? We didn't know, but those close to her had a sense that it wasn't going to be long.

> Thanx God for my family. Had a chance to go to the shops with Grandma, Aunty Wendy, Melissa, Kyah, and Mum. I love how close we are!! I love how we always end up at the shops! HaHaHa. ☺[4]

> I thank God for family and how special they are to me. Thank you God for Melissa and how I feel so close to her. Thank you for her family and how special they are to me. I thank God for a family—both the Allder family and the Dudley family that stick together through thick and thin.[5]

Soon after BJ was diagnosed, Wendy (Jacque's older sister) made a beautiful quilt that BJ could use. It was embossed with the words "love" and "faith" affirming BJ's emphases in life. Being gifted at quilting, she also made a quilted rug to go over the coffin at the committal service just a few days prior to the service. Sewn into the quilt were the words "Under His Sky" with several stars surrounding the words. Draping this beautiful quilt over the coffin gave the sombre looking coffin a very "BJ" look about it. These were special gifts that we continue to treasure.

But there were two and half years together before those last few moments. We are grateful for the Australian social security system that allowed BJ to go on to a "disability pension." The Australian government paid her considerably more than she was paid as a missionary and also paid most of the medical expenses too! Praise the Lord! When BJ received her pension card in the mail, she excitedly phoned both grandmas and said, "Hey Grandma, we can go to the movies at the pensioner rate! We can hang out together." This of course was received with great amusement and joy. We are grateful for godly grandparents who prayed for her constantly and loved having BJ around to "hang out" when she could. Some of the

---

4. Ibid., Aug 9, 2010.
5. Ibid., June 10, 2011.

sweetest things written to BJ in notes, etc., were from her grandparents. She treasured them.

> Thanx God for Mum!! Grandma A and Grandma D! What wonderful mothers I have in my life!! ☺ Examples of mothers, wives, of Godly women! They all do *so* much for me!! They all mean so much to me!! Thank you God for this wonderful blessing. May I follow in their footsteps!!⁶

Jacque's mum wrote of BJ:

> The other day I read where friends are flowers in the garden of life. Well Belinda (BJ), you must have the largest garden in the world with flowers of all shapes and sizes and colours, all facing you now, but when you go to heaven they will turn to the sky with a smile knowing some day they will join you up there. My love. Grandma.⁷

The many times Jacque did the "chemo run" with BJ were special mother/daughter times. Despite the treatments they had fun times together while they waited for blood test results and awaiting final clearance to have chemo that day. Trips to Max Brenner chocolate specialty store and wandering through various departments stores that were accessible from the hospital in the city were great times together.

> Mum! Today is Mothers' Day! I love my Mum! It has been a real blessing to be here with her again. She is such a blessing to me—man—the things she does for me (I probably don't even know them all). She is such a giving mother! . . . In the last few days we have become even closer and as she takes this term off, my prayer is that we will grow closer still. May we grow closer in You together . . . She really keeps us all together and for that I am so grateful. I thank you for all her amazing gifts as well as mothering duties—amazing host, huge behind the scenes worker, her love for church and music—which she has passed on, her integrity, her cooking, her care (even that edge of red hair temper—and not letting us get away with stuff)—good upbringing, her love and inclusion of my friends, her willingness to help at any time, her hard working ethic. For all that you are Mum, I love you!! I thank God for giving me you as my Mum!!⁸

6. Ibid., May 8, 2010.
7. June Dudley, personal correspondence, Jan 16, 2012.
8. BJ diary, May 8, 2011.

There was one very special family occasion that we hoped and prayed BJ would be able to attend—that of Tim's wedding to Carine. The target date was April 15, 2011, and with a number of international and interstate visitors being present there was no flexibility in the date. Fifteen months into BJ's chemo treatment and we hoped that no complications would arise to prevent her attending. However, circumstances became difficult for BJ. There was a change in chemotherapy and one of the side effects was the eruption of severe acne over the face and other parts of the body. BJ despaired over that possibility until the doctor assured her that the appearance of the acne would not be until after the wedding. It would take time for the drug to manifest its side effects. BJ took that as good news!

All appeared to be going well until about a week before the wedding when BJ had a major fever, indicating an infection. This meant a trip to the hospital where she was required to stay for tests until the doctors found the source of infection and could treat it appropriately. Circumstances were not looking good for BJ's attendance at the wedding. This was discouraging news for everyone, although we kept hoping that she would be OK. After being in hospital a week, the doctors located the infection on the Wednesday afternoon—the wedding was scheduled for early Friday afternoon. Her dear friend Pastor David was officiating at the wedding ceremony. What a disappointment to miss her brother's wedding as well as miss the opportunity to see Pastor David.

Would she make it out of hospital in time? BJ's oncologist kept on assuring BJ that she would "get her to the wedding somehow"! However, the doctors were not prepared to release BJ until they were sure that she was responding to the antibiotic. So we prayed, hoped, and anxiously checked with the hospital every few hours. A "day pass" from the hospital was a possibility, but the fever needed to come down! BJ began her antibiotic treatment late Wednesday night, and we prayed that it would do what it needed to do and bring her fever down. Thursday evening, even while BJ was connected to the IV drips, the discipleship girls went to the hospital and prepared BJ for going to the wedding. They painted her nails, prepared makeup, etc., and took care of the things that ladies need to do before attending a big event. Everything was being done to ensure that BJ could get to the wedding.

Friday morning, with the wedding scheduled for 2 p.m., the doctors gave BJ a day pass to leave hospital to attend the wedding! We had strict instructions to take her temperature regularly. If it increased, I was to return her to the hospital. I raced to the hospital (a forty-minute drive from home) and by mid-morning BJ and I were driving home to get ready for a wedding! Praise the Lord. This was a special family moment for all of us. Surprisingly, or perhaps not so for those who had prayed so fervently, BJ did not have to return to the hospital after the wedding. I'm not sure what would have happened if her temperature had risen. I have a sneaking suspicion BJ would have ignored it until well after the wedding and celebrations. This was family, and the focus was to be on Tim and Carine. She would not have wanted it any other way!

The wedding was a beautiful garden wedding and everything went off without a hitch. Perhaps the highlight for BJ though was when Carine, rather than throw her bouquet of flowers over her shoulder to a number of waiting single young ladies as is the tradition, went to BJ and presented her with the bouquet. This symbol of love and respect by Carine moved us all very deeply and truly expressed a love for BJ that was indeed very special. It felt right, and with tears and hugs BJ gratefully took the bouquet and the expressions of love that came with the presentation. We will not forget that beautiful expression by Carine to her sister-in-law.

Mel, BJ's best friend, and husband, Jim, and their children have become family to us over the last three or four years. Mel was always considered like another daughter to us, and when Jim came on the scene, he graciously joined the family too. Mel had a level of understanding of BJ and a relationship that can be genuinely described as "soul mates." By December 2011 it was clear that there was a steady deterioration in BJ's health to the point that even the immediate future was uncertain for BJ. Mel intuitively knew that to gather a group of friends and family that would join BJ in worship under the stars would be of great encouragement to her. December 11, 2011, was set as the date and Mel put out the word in the hope that some would come—and come they did! Jenny and Rebecca Karmas came from Sydney and Derene Els travelled from New Zealand just for the occasion, while many locals came to share the time. The hope was that we could meet outside under a starry night in tune with BJ's theme of "Under His Sky." However, the weather did not cooperate so Mitch got to work with Simon Kohlman and transformed the Student Commons room at NTC into a beautiful "starry" expanse through special lighting effects. BJ was not well enough to go to church that morning, but we managed to get her to the event in the Student Commons room that evening.

> Wow! What can I say! Thanx God! It was my "Under His Sky" night that Melinda had organised. Sausage sizzle, worship and prayer. It was amazing!! I thank you Lord for amazing friends who worked so hard to pull it off—and who even thought of the idea. I thank you Lord for all of the support of all of the people that came out! *So* lovely!! Sitting there amongst family and friends praising God. *Awesome*!! The prayers were so precious too. I thank God for the community of believers that is *always* lifting me up in prayer.[9]

Events such as this were of great encouragement, not just to BJ, but also to the rest of the family. There appeared to be a deepening understanding of our journey as we spent time in worship. We did not have answers—just a sense of being in God's presence in worship. Worship songs were an integral part of such times. Many of BJ's journal entries quote the words of a worship song as it would speak to her through her daily devotions. Remembering past events where we had seen God at work; marvelling at God's creative touch upon our lives; the many people with whom we had contact; and simply to revel in God's presence became precious times together.

> "And the Holy Spirit helps us in our distress, for we don't even know what we should pray for, nor how we should pray. But the Holy Spirit prays for us with groanings that cannot be expressed in words" (Rom 8:26–27). Prayer!! It has become so special and this above verse is where I sit most of the time—not sure how to pray, but just coming before the Father! I thank God for times spent praying with friends. It is so important and it means so much. Thanks also for the many prayers for me that are going out around the world.[10]

> An amazing day! I don't even know what to write! Surprise visit for the day (Wow!) from Yvonne, Kylie and Jared Harris, Malae and Grace Sega. We did our house church—amazing! Just sang through songs we used to sing back in the Birrong days! *So* special!! We are family. We spent the day in the lounge room all day—singing, crying, praying, laughing, reminiscing, playing games, and of course—*eating*!! It was such a blessed day—a real God moment—perfect group, perfect timing—one of the most special days of my life. And great to spend time, real time, God time, with family!! That particular group of people (including the Good family, Grandma and my immediate family) are my family!! Thank

---

9. BJ diary, Dec 11, 2011.
10. Ibid., Nov 24, 2011.

you *so* much God for this family! Thanx for allowing them to come up to Brisbane. What a blessing! Thanx for this special day—will treasure it forever!![11]

By December 2011, with a sense of gratefulness, BJ began to prepare for her passing by sorting through a lot of her special possessions. BJ was a "keeper" and little knickknacks she had been given over the years were still safely stored in my garage. I think every birthday card or note of encouragement she had received from before her high school days had been kept and appreciated. I think this is why BJ was herself a great giver of notes of encouragement. She had been blessed herself by notes from people who cared enough to send something. In January 2012 she began to go through box upon box of her knickknacks. She did not have the strength to lift things so Mitch and I would drag boxes into the lounge room. When she had the energy she would work through the contents with Jacque. It was time to give away mementos to friends and family.

> Thanx God for the joy of giving. I love giving gifts and it has been so fun to be able to give out "memories" of me to my friends and family. It's very hard at the same time because I don't have a lot—but fun at the same time. It was fun to be at the shops today and buy Jenny some star earrings! I've always loved birthdays and stuff and thinking what to give people. It's kinda weird though too at the moment because I am not gone yet! Giving my stuff away—so surreal—and if I end up making it longer, it will be like—"Hey, I need my stuff back!" Hahaha. The special moments and memories that are still being created are such fun. I just don't want these days to end—even though I know they will! And I am at peace with that. But this is so fun—I want to make sure that I have given all my gifts!![12]

As the pressure began to build with BJ's failing health, it was important that the many questions raised by many of BJ's friends were addressed. Jacque and I were in no position, either emotionally or time wise, to take this task on. For some two and a half years, BJ had faithfully texted, Facebooked, e-mailed, phoned . . . for friends situated literally around the world. Most times that I drove BJ to hospital appointments, the entire forty-minute journey was spent with BJ texting friends, and letting people know what was happening. Now it was a time for a different approach. Pastor David,

---

11. Ibid., Jan 15, 2012.
12. Ibid., Jan 28, 2012.

himself known as "Mr. Networker," offered to administer a Facebook page where regular updates could be posted. This was an absolute "Godsend" for us. We could talk with David and he would then convey the latest via the Facebook page, "Under His Sky," to the many friends who wanted to keep in touch. David is gifted in writing sensitive but informative posts that were appreciated by everyone. This was an especially significant ministry to us as a family. His post announcing the passing of BJ is typical of David's beautiful style:

> Dear friends, we grieve this morning the passing of our beloved Belinda, quietly, peacefully, her mum and dad with her, and with her last breath, a sweet smile. Our hearts ache, we weep, yet, we are buoyed beyond measure that BJ is in the presence of the One who created her, redeemed her, transformed her, used her for His glory in the work of the Kingdom, accomplishing His purposes on earth & in the hearts of many. What a privilege to have journeyed with this dynamic, gregarious, spiritual giant. We will rejoice and be glad! This is day that the Lord has made![13]

It is difficult to single out members of the extended family for special mention, because all have been significant supporters to us at one time or another. However, Jacque's younger sister, Bronwyn, and husband, Mark, have been particularly supportive on a number of levels. As Christians we have found them to be amazingly understanding and nurturing of what we have been going through as a family. Mark and Bronwyn identified with BJ's missionary heart as they have spent a number of years overseas teaching. They have also been extremely generous in assisting at key times of financial stress—all unsolicited, but gratefully received as an encouragement from the Lord. We know they have given sacrificially!

> I don't think I have thanked God yet for Uncle Mark's song. Wow!! He wrote a "Goodbye Belinda Goodbye" song. It makes me cry every time I listen to it! How very special—and it's on my Facebook as a link to YouTube. Everyone loves it! Thank you Lord.[14]

Mark is a talented musician/songwriter and we are grateful that he put his creative talents to work. He wrote both the words and music of a song that he professionally recorded and it was played at BJ's committal and celebration services. We continue to find the song very moving.

---

13. David Harris, "Under His Sky" Facebook page (accessed Feb 15, 2012), http://www.facebook.com/UnderHisSky.

14. BJ diary, Feb 1, 2012.

The Family Journey

Goodbye, Belinda, Goodbye©

BJ, I can't believe you're leaving. Goodbye, my friend, we are all so grieving.
So much promise in your hands, so much faith wells in your eyes.
So much hope holds every heartbeat, now such sorrow fills our sighs
"Well done" Jesus says "my good and faithful friend. Enter into heaven your race is near an end."
You ran with so much dignity, you run with head held high, now run toward the One you serve His arms are open wide.
Belinda, goodbye. Belinda, goodbye. Belinda, goodbye. Belinda, goodbye. Belinda, goodbye.
With so much promise in your hands, so much faith wells in your eyes
So much hope holds every heartbeat, now such sorrow fills our sighs
Belinda, goodbye. Belinda, goodbye.
I can't say "Good bye," so I'll say "See you later on," in the twinkling of an eye we'll all be singing heaven's song
There's a star up in the heavens that has your name BJ, so as long as we live under His sky your name will never fade
Belinda, goodbye, you're under His sky. Belinda, goodbye. We're under His sky
There's a star up in the heavens, has your name "BJ." And when we look up to the sky you're never far away
Belinda, goodbye. Belinda, goodbye. Belinda, goodbye. Belinda, goodbye. We're under His sky. Belinda, goodbye. We're under His sky.[15]

    BJ faced her last days with courage and grace. Jacque, Mitch and I had several conversations with BJ about her funeral. She had firm ideas about what should happen and we tried to honour her requests. First, she did not want the time of gathering to be dominated by sadness and sorrow. She wanted her favourite worship songs sung (which she quickly listed) and a time of worship that would focus on God's faithfulness and goodness. BJ had a peace about what was happening to her and she would share that with her many visitors. Often, visitors would come with the questions that we attribute to those with a terminal illness, wondering where God is in all that was taking place. It was BJ who ministered hope and peace to them, rather than the other way around. One of the key things BJ would do when visitors came with perplexing questions was to sit down with them and watch

---

15. Mark Oakey, lyrics and music, "Belinda, Goodbye," Jan 2012.

A Hope-Filled Journey Under His Sky

Louie Giglio's two-sermon series "Hope When Life Hurts the Most" from his "Passion" series. She must have watched those sermons twenty or thirty times as she helped friends through the crisis of faith and troubling questions of "why." Louie Giglio articulates well this journey where life takes unexpected turns and we can only anchor our lives in Jesus and the cross of Christ for stability and balance. We decided to use portions of these two sermons by Giglio in the celebration service to help focus the service on God's amazing provision for us in Christ.

Our second point of discussion was what we should do by way of a funeral service and committal. I don't think we ever really thought seriously about having a burial. Nowadays in Australia cremations are becoming much more common for a number of practical reasons. BJ was happy with cremation. The greater question for me was whether we should have a private service of committal restricted to the immediate family and closest of friends, and then an open service of celebration for the many friends of BJ. I liked the idea a lot. I did not know how Jacque and I were going to cope with a very public committal service. Both of us were exhausted both physically and emotionally, not just from the demands of nursing BJ, but also from our demanding jobs that appeared to be relentless in their demands even in the midst of our personal pressures. In theory it seemed quite a reasonable thing to have a private committal service since BJ lived such a public life. However, the sticking point was who to exclude. As BJ began to recite names of people that she would feel uncomfortable excluding, we soon realised that it was not a practical solution to have a private service. Her sense of inclusion, the many who had gone out of their way to honour or bless BJ in some way through her illness, and BJ's commitment to transparency and authentic relationships, all pointed us in the direction of an open committal service. Jacque and I would just need to take it as it came. In one sense I was so proud of BJ for wanting that. She expressed beautifully the welcoming nature of the gospel and her high value that people mattered to God and to her. She did not want anyone to be marginalised.

Of course there was no doubt as to who would conduct the service, if he was willing—her pastor, David Harris—mentor, pastor, friend and ministry colleague. With that, most of the major decisions had been made with BJ. We were happy to carry out her wishes to the best of our ability. It was a way of saying to BJ, "We love you. We respect you. We honour you for your commitment to Christ, to family and the church." There are no right and wrong answers to these questions, but the decisions we made for our context felt right.

The committal service was conducted at the Great Southern Garden of Remembrance, Mt. Cotton, just a few kilometres from NTC, and the celebration service was conducted at the Meadowlands Church of the Nazarene. This was the only Nazarene church building large enough to accommodate the expected crowd and it was in this congregation that BJ was involved in leading of worship services. Jacque and Mitch were part of the music team there each Sunday, and so it was a natural choice of venue. Knowing that there were many people around Australia and overseas who would not be able to attend the service in person, Tim and Mitch organised the live streaming of the celebration service. Tim called in a number of favours from work associates to get the necessary equipment to make it a high quality broadcast, and Mitch worked hard on putting together a very competent musical team for the event. This was something that each member of the family involved felt honoured to be a part.

BJ wanted her close friends from Sydney, whom she had discipled, to be involved in the music, along with the music team from the Brisbane area. We were able to do this by having the music team from Sydney involved in the committal service and the Brisbane music team involved in the celebration service. Both teams did an awesome job!

I will always be grateful that BJ had time to prepare for her passing, and we had time to prepare as well. BJ was intentional about having focussed conversations with most of the extended family, one on one. I will probably never know the content of some of those conversations, but I think that they were each important conversations. My heart goes out to those who experience the sudden passing of a loved one. Not having the opportunity to say some things that needed to be said would have been devastating for us. But then, what was said? Often it was simply the opportunity to tell each other that we love each other, appreciate who they are and how they faced this situation with grace and dignity. BJ gave Jacque and me permission to read her "Thank you" diaries in the last few days of her life. What a special gift to us as we read some really touching things about how often she thought of us and appreciated us.

> Thanx God for my amazing Mum!! She is taking care of me in ways that are above and beyond—even having to shower me! She has decided to take a term off work to be my full time carer. Wow!! I can't imagine how hard this is for Mum and Dad. I feel for them!

> It must be *so* hard to watch this happen to me. I can't begin to imagine—in many ways I think it is harder for them. I thank you God for their strength!! They just continue to support me. Never have they told me off, or what to do, but it's been a walking alongside, carrying the burden together and total understanding of who I am (e.g. needing people around, finding rest hard, letting me go out etc. etc.) Their love for me is so evident and I am truly grateful for my amazing parents. Thank you Lord for giving me such Godly parents—the way they also understand that I just need to live each day for God and see what happens for the future (which so many people just don't get—but they do—and that is their testimony too). I thank you Lord, how my parents have just accepted my amazing close friends as family. It is so special!! Again Lord, I don't know how to put in words but thanx for my amazing, self-sacrificing, God loving parents!![16]

We needed to hear that. We needed to hear that we were successfully enabling BJ to live her final days the way she wanted. We needed to know that we were connecting at a soul level. When Jacque massaged BJ's feet every day the last month or so; when Mitch or I carried her to the bathroom several times a day; when one or more of us spent time playing a table game with her in the late night hours; when we all played host to over 253 different people in the last month of BJ's life; when one of us would sit with her for an hour or two at a time; we needed to know that we were connecting. BJ was able to communicate that to us, and this was a profound blessing. I thank God that BJ was a verbal person who expressed these thoughts along the way. She did not leave these things unsaid.

One of BJ's wishes which we were unable to fulfil was to have her Thai "mum" and her Thai "sister" attend the celebration service in Brisbane. We pulled out all stops to try and make that happen. Right from the start we were up against a very tight time schedule and the Immigration Department, primarily in Thailand, was not sensitive to those time constraints. I think our Thai friends also saw the possibility of travelling to Australia as something beyond their comprehension. Despite the assurances of finances and guarantees they were not able to secure appropriate travel documents. We were frustrated! This made a trip to Thailand by us at some point an important thing to do. We wanted to bring closure for ourselves as well for our Thai friends. We did hear of a memorial service for BJ conducted in Maetang by BJ's ministry colleagues soon after her passing. I would have

---

16. BJ diary, Jan 11, 2012.

loved to have been there but none of the family were in a position, emotionally, physically or financially to do this. Missionary colleague Lisa Lehman also organised a memorial service for BJ in Bangkok. It seemed that many appreciated BJ's ministry and wanted to thank God for her life and ministry.

A decision that we waited until after BJ's death to consider was what to do with her ashes. Right from the start we felt that it would be appropriate to take some of the ashes back to Thailand, a place BJ really considered home. BJ had indicated to us that she would like that to be done if possible. I also wanted to find a place in Australia that we could do the same—a place that we could visit from time to time. What amazed me was the incredible cost of placing ashes in a memorial garden associated with a crematorium or cemetery in Australia. We know for certain that BJ would be horrified if we had spent that kind of money on a name plaque in a brick wall somewhere or a rose bush in a garden. After much thought, discussion and debate we decided to approach Nazarene Theological College, Brisbane, about dedicating a garden and placing a small memorial in her honour in that garden. Throughout her illness, BJ was a vital member of the NTC community. She was the first TESOL graduate of the New Horizons School of English (a department of NTC) and she completed her master of arts at NTC 2011. She was involved in many social events on campus, and connected with many of the students, and taught in the free English programme. It seemed a natural connection to make. We are grateful that NTC agreed to our request and we went ahead and prepared the garden and the memorial. In a quiet ceremony, attended by many of BJ's friends as well as family, we sprinkled ashes in the garden and placed a small monument in her memory.

It was agreed amongst the family that we should take a portion of BJ's ashes to Thailand, and that we would all travel to Thailand on the first anniversary of her passing to do that. Over a period of several months we worked with church leadership in Thailand to ensure culturally appropriate things were done. Our major concern was that we wanted to leave some of BJ's ashes in a place that became home to her. Even though BJ was an Australian and spent the last two and a half years living in Brisbane, Thailand was home. We wanted to acknowledge that and while, for cultural reasons we did not have a public ceremony of laying ashes in Thailand, Jacque and I did so very privately. We did plant a tree in memory of BJ in front of the house she lived in at the Maetang Tribal Children's Home. BJ's ministry colleague Siripawn found a small monument to place in the garden alongside the tree. The little ceremony outside BJ's Thailand home was attended by just a handful of close Thai friends, and people she had adopted as "family" there. Along with Jacque and me, Tim, Carine, Mitch, Mariko and Aaron travelled from Australia to be present in Maetang on February 15, 2013, one year after BJ's passing. Jacque and I stayed in the house that BJ had called home for seven years. The house was still filled with touches of BJ and it was a special moment of remembering for Jacque and me. Several people gave financial gifts to us with the expressed purpose of helping us "take BJ home." How grateful we are for Christian friends!

One of the most difficult questions that often gets asked by a new acquaintance as we chat is "How many children do you have?" Up until recently we have both answered "three." This then inevitably leads to a discussion about BJ and her recent passing. Up until very recently, I have felt that to not include BJ in the answer would be to dishonour her memory. I overheard Jacque talking to her hairdresser the other day. When she was asked how many children we have, her response was, "Two boys." The conversation was then about the boys and all that they are doing. We are proud of them and want them to know that they are loved. The hairdresser chatted about her children as well. The emphasis was on the living; the issues we face now. No mention was made of BJ and the pain we still feel each day. And I felt that was OK. Perhaps this is a sign that we are beginning to heal. We are no longer dominated by the crushing burden of loss whereby every conversation and waking moment must include some expression of our pain. We are learning to cherish the memories of our precious daughter in ways that do not produce a stabbing pain to the heart. We are learning to deal with our loss. It is time to acknowledge that each family member had put BJ and her needs front and centre out of necessity, but now it is time to thank God for what we still have, and give thanks for our beautiful family.

Perhaps, we are moving on with our lives. Perhaps we are at last learning to respond to Jesus' invitation:

> Come to me, all you that are weary and carrying heavy burdens, and I will give you rest. Take my yoke upon you, and learn from me; for I am gentle and humble in heart, and you will find rest for your souls. For my yoke is easy, and my burden is light. (Matt 11:28–30)

As we look up into the night sky these days we think of the star named after BJ that her discipleship girls gifted her in December 2011. We think of an amazing daughter who served Jesus "under his sky," and we give thanks to God for the amazing privilege of being BJ's parents.

Chapter 7

Faith Reflections

ALL THESE EVENTS ARE a long way from the time that Jacque and I stood in front of the Inala Church of the Nazarene in 1978 and dedicated our three-week-old "precious bundle" of joy to the Lord. As proud parents of our firstborn, the words of commitment that we made as my father, Rev. George Allder, officiated at BJ's dedication, didn't have the poignancy that they have now! But then I guess that is always the way in such ceremonies. Whether it is a commitment in marriage or the dedication of children to God, we can never really anticipate what that commitment will look like later in life. All we know is that we were prepared to say "yes," and remain faithful to that commitment when the time of testing came. We reminded ourselves of that moment of dedication when we farewelled BJ on her missionary journey. And again we were reminded of our vow when the time came to release our precious daughter into the arms of her Saviour.

So here I am over four years after BJ's passing and our grieving process continues. As a pastor I have been in the homes of probably hundreds of grieving people. I know the theory regarding the process of grief, and I have been a part of seminars designed to assist us clergy in dealing with grieving people. Nevertheless, when the loss is so personal and the pain so intense, the theory takes on a whole new depth of meaning. I felt out of my depth and uncertain of what to do that would adequately bring comfort to my family and friends. Others ultimately began to set the agenda in this. For example, BJ's friends in Sydney, who were unable to make the celebration service in February, organised a time of remembering on May 4, 2012; BJ's birthday. The Australia Southern District Church of the Nazarene very generously assisted financially in order for Jacque and me to be present. The time of remembering was done in the context of a worship time which reflected BJ's priority in life. While these times were not easy to attend, they did form a part of the healing journey for us.

A time of sabbatical in Florida (USA) twelve months after BJ's passing, has been of inestimable value. With a project to write up something of BJ's story along with my personal journey through this time of grief, the opportunity to get away from the normal pressures of ministry, and the privilege of having the time to physically exercise regularly, all have assisted in my spiritual journey toward healing. Jacque and I have cried together, laughed together, and made new friends. During our sabbatical we attended a small Nazarene church in central Florida who embraced us and allowed us to heal, with no expectations placed upon us. We found likeminded people to "do life together" and have been nurtured as a result.

There are times when we identify with Abraham's trudging up the mountain with Isaac and the makings of a sacrifice at God's request (Genesis 22). What was God expecting of Abraham? The request did not make a whole lot of sense. It seems that simple obedience, in faith, was what God was seeking. While we may struggle in our way of thinking about what Abraham was asked to do, we also wondered at the oddities of life and the feelings when, what we experienced, did not make sense. Why was God silent when one of his children, who had become an amazing servant of the Lord, was in desperate need? I don't think for a moment that God was the author of BJ's cancer. But I do think that in the midst of the storm, God was asking us to trust him. We did not know the future, and given what unfolded, I am glad that we didn't! We just needed to respond in obedience and trust—knowing that God was with us. Did Jacque and I want it some other way? Of course! We would have loved to have a family where our daughter lived a long life close by us, married, had children so we could enjoy the extended family even more. But, despite the cost, we would not want to change any of BJ's decisions. She shone for Jesus in remarkable ways.

A particularly comforting Scripture for me through this time has been:

> Are not two sparrows sold for a penny? Yet *not one of them will fall to the ground apart from your Father*. And even the hairs of your head are all counted. So do not be afraid; you are more value than many sparrows. (Matt 10:29–31 NRSV, emphasis mine)

The amazing sense of God's presence in the midst of all that unfolded, allowed us, as a family, to carry on. I "heard" out of this verse: *Not one of these precious little sparrows will fall to the earth without the Father being present. How much more will he be present with you in your devastation?* Rather than Abraham's response to Isaac, "God will provide," our response was, "God knows! He is with us. That has to be sufficient." This was no easy or glib response to make. It was often made through clenched teeth and with a bewilderment that appeared to almost crush us. But, God has been with us! His presence has brought comfort and enough strength for the moment.

There is an open-endedness to this that is often disconcerting. There is no closure to the troubling questions. Rather there is a growing realisation that the questions raised are almost irrelevant, no matter how pressing they may appear to be initially. I am reminded of the Bible story of Job who suffered greatly, even though he was acknowledged as a righteous man. Good living had apparently not gone well for him! His friends, well-intentioned as they might have been, raised questions of Job's integrity, and of God's justice. These questions reflect the preconceived notions of the questioner, and reveal an inadequate heuristic. These questions are, at best, uncomfortable, but often in the dark times of suffering, haunt us and drive us into despair. The experience shatters the meaning constructs that we have developed to this point in time. The pain of this is deep and traumatic.

Listen to portions of Job's journey:

> O that my vexation were weighed, and all my calamity laid in the balances! For then it would be heavier than the sand of the sea; therefore my words have been rash. For the arrows of the Almighty are in me; my spirit drinks their poison; the terrors of God are arrayed against me. Teach me, and I will be silent; make me understand how I have gone wrong. How forceful are honest words! (Job 6:2–4; 24 NRSV)

The assumption of Job's friends is that Job is guilty of some sin and that God only rewards those who have not sinned. Job is painfully aware that he is the subject of ridicule as observers note that his good living has not prospered him. They assume that Job harbours secret sin, known only to himself and God.

> How long will you torment me, and break me in pieces with words? These ten times you have cast reproach upon me; are you not ashamed to wrong me? And even if it is true that I have erred, my error remains with me, and make my humiliation an argument against me. Know then that God has put me in the wrong, and closed his net around me. Even when I cry out, "Violence!" I am not answered; I call aloud, but there is no justice. He has walled up my way so that I cannot pass, and he has set darkness upon my paths. He has stripped my glory from me and taken the crown

from my head. He breaks me down on every side, and I am gone, he has uprooted my hope like a tree. (Job 19:2-10 NRSV)

Yet, in spite of this Job says:

> I know that my Redeemer lives, and that at the last he will stand upon the earth, and after my skins has been thus destroyed, then in my flesh *I shall see God, who I shall see on my side*, and my eyes shall behold, and not another. (Job 19:25-27a NRSV, emphasis mine)

This unshakable faith continued to be battered by suffering and the growing irrelevancy of Job's friends' questions and unhelpful advice. Job appeared anchored in two realities that remained sure throughout the trauma. First, his conviction that God was his ultimate Redeemer. Second, that he stood with a clear conscience before his God.

> As God lives, who has taken away my right, and the Almighty, who has made my soul bitter, as long as my breath is in me and the spirit of God is in my nostril, my lips will not speak falsehood, and my tongue will not utter deceit. Far be it from me to say that you are right; until I die I will not put away my integrity from me. I hold fast my righteousness, and will not let it go; my heart does not reproach me for any of my days. (Job 27:2-6 NRSV)

The story of Job draws near to a close when he is caught up in worship of this God who appeared to have treated him so shabbily. Job, himself had complained bitterly about his lot in life. He had failed to comprehend how all the pieces of his circumstances fit together in any meaningful way. In his confusion, pain, and anguish, God questioned Job, rather than Job questioning God. Job 38-39 is a litany of questions from God that points to the frailty and temporality of Job. Overwhelmed by the majesty and glory of a Creative God, Job's response was:

> See, I am of small account; what shall I answer you? I have spoken once, and I will not answer; twice, but will proceed no further . . . I have uttered what I did not understand, things too wonderful for me, which I did not know . . . I had heard of you by the hearing of the ear, but now my eye sees you; therefore, I despise myself and repent in dust and ashes. (Job 40:4-5; 42:3b; 42:5-6 NRSV)

It appears that Job's encounter with God was enough. His anchor of God as his Redeemer held in the midst of the unanswered questions. It is okay to leave the questions unanswered or perhaps be left with open-ended answers. Having this Creator God journey with Job in the suffering was sufficient.

Living life in the present and thanking God for what is right now has been a hard lesson to learn. The opportunity to simply "be" while we anguish over our own ill health or that of a loved one does not come easily. I want to fix it, or wait expectantly for the time when our prayers are answered in the way I thought they should be answered. BJ has taught me much about being present in the "now" of suffering. I am encouraged to wait in the experience of suffering to discern God's grace at work; to "lean in" to suffering rather than recoil from it.

> Blessing the Lord at all times invites us to live fully in the "now" of our lives and to commit to authentic prayer that does not regard God as a kind of benevolent Santa Claus but as a loving parent who wants only the very best for us but will not remove the risk of being fully human. After all, the incarnation was God's great risk as the creative Word who was with the Creator at the beginning of all things "became flesh and lived among us" (John 1:14) ... If we will give time to the pain, be present to the harsh experience, we will be given grace to see as God sees and find perspective so that we do not lose heart.[1]

It has always been intriguing to read the biblical accounts of Jesus healing the sick. There are times when it appears that Jesus heals all those seeking healing (Matt 15:29–31). Other times he just appeared to heal the one or two only (John 5); of all the death and dying around Jesus, why Lazarus, and not a host of other people? The answer appears to be in understanding God's greater purpose of revealing his glory in specific ways.

> Did I not tell you that if you believed, you would see the glory of God? (John 11:40 NRSV)

In this instance God's glory was revealed through the healing of Lazarus. Are there other ways in which God's glory is revealed apart from physical healing and physical resurrection? This is the bigger question. To answer this there is a need to explore what we mean by "God's glory." There is a temptation to think in terms of God's self-indulgence or simply to honour oneself. Is that what God is doing here? If we are to embed this experience in the whole narrative of Scripture, we see Scripture telling the story of God's revelation of himself, and his redemptive work to save humankind.

---

1. Elizabeth Canham, "Do Not Lose Heart," *Weavings* 27 (2012) 42.

Showing God's glory is a revelation of God's nature. This is part and parcel of God's expression of himself. The focus is not on physical healing per se, rather on the opportunity to reveal his loving nature in the course of redemptive history.

My prayers are now framed differently. No longer are they narrowly focussed on a self-centred appeal to ease my suffering or those of the one in the midst of a physical trauma. Rather my prayers have turned to seeking God to reveal his nature in and through the person or situation. This is a harder prayer to pray when I think I know how God should answer. I have had to confess (like Job) my arrogance at thinking I knew the solution to my request. I can envisage a positive future, but it was on my terms. My praying is now done in a spirit of worship and listening. I have been conscious of the two seemingly opposite tendencies to which I am tempted to drift. First that of arrogantly asserting the way in which God ought to answer my prayers. "This is what I want, Lord, and You can do this!" Second, the drift to a fatalistic determinism that assumes that "things will be what they will be"; that we simply pray to show our need for God, but he will work according to some narrowly defined plan of which I know little. Fringer and Lane's book *The Theology of Luck* has helped me wrestle with this big question.[2]

In a sermon, "Hope when Life Hurts the Most,"[3] Louie Giglio speaks of our lives being a "megaphone for God's glory" as we allow God to work in and through our suffering. Such experiences can become a platform from which God can show his loving nature and his ultimate redemptive purposes—sometimes through healing and sometimes through the suffering. God's glory can be revealed in desperate circumstances. It is in the extremes of the cross of Christ that God's love is shown the most vividly. God's glory can show us ultimate reality if we are not too eager, or arrogant, or frightened of suffering, to frame our prayers in terms of the revelation of God's glory. It is in the darkness that God's light shines ever more brightly and in the turmoil of suffering that God's grace is amplified to a dull of hearing people. It is the opportunity to turn our attention to ultimate realities.

The Apostle Paul challenges the Thessalonians:

> We do not want you to be uninformed, brothers and sisters, about those who have died, *so that you may not grieve as others do who have no hope.* (1 Thess 4:13 NRSV)

---

2. Rob Fringer and Jeff Lane, *The Theology of Luck* (Kansas City: Beacon Hill, 2015).
3. Louie Giglio, "Hope when Life Hurts the Most," Passion Conference 2009.

Faith Reflections

What does it look like to "grieve with hope"? Some can be tempted to think that a Christian view is to dismiss grief as something that only those with no hope indulge. The laments of the psalmist go a long way to correcting that understanding. However, lament alone does not point to hope even if the expression of grief can be cathartic in the short term. Boersma, in interpreting Gregory of Nyssa, says:

> The pastor has the duty to take into account the theological problem of sin, which Gregory sees in the passion of grief that overshadows the hope of eternal life. He believes it is the fundamental duty to comfort his congregation with the rational hope of the resurrection—a hope that is temporarily clouded as a result of grief.[4]

In commenting on Jesus at the grave of Lazarus, Boersma continues:

> Jesus has been teaching about the resurrection, and when he weeps he is about to raise his friend from the dead. Thus, Jesus is unlikely to be weeping because he misses his friend, Lazarus. Jesus' grief is of a much deeper kind than ours: I suspect it is grief over Martha and Mary's incomprehension; it is grief over the lack of faith of several bystanders; and it is grief over the power that death, as the last enemy, still exercises. In short, Jesus grieves the power that sin and death still hold but that he has come to defeat.[5]

I return to the journey of Job who found an anchor in the midst of the open-endedness of life and suffering; an unshakable faith in his God as Redeemer and Saviour. I thank God that this side of Easter I can celebrate Christ as our Redeemer, Servant King, even if it is through tears of loss and pain.

I must confess that when the pressure is on, the pain most intense and, with despair knocking at the door, finding hope is a challenge. There are many things to distract the focus. I find the examples of Elijah (1 Kgs 19) and the disciple Peter (Matt 14:22–33) helpful at this point. Elijah, swamped in despair and discouragement, wondered why he was still living. He stood at the mouth of the cave where he had been hiding and witnessed the earthquake, the wind and the fire. It wasn't until he turned his focus from these that in the sheer silence he heard the voice of God. Likewise the disciple Peter was invited by Jesus to walk on the water. Peter climbed out

---

4. Hans Boersma, "Numbed with Grief: Gregory of Nyssa on Bereavement and Hope," *Journal of Spiritual Formation and Soul Care* 7 (2014) 57.

5. Ibid., 58.

of the boat and then when he looked at the waves and the storm, he began to doubt and sink. It wasn't a focus on the storm and the pressures that were about them that brought a sense of hope, but looking to and listening for the still presence of the One who journeyed with them through the pressures.

There is a temptation to focus on the storm and be mesmerised by the chaos and destruction all about. However, I am learning to take to heart Jesus' words in Matthew 10:29–31 once more. It is a journey that we travel, learning to be at ease with open-endedness and mystery. The assurance is that God journeys with us. What motivates God to be present on this journey is a deep and abiding love for his creation that is doggedly persistent. This love is big enough to allow questions that are expressed in the anguish of suffering. This love is patient enough to walk with us through these dark valleys of confusion and despair, until we find the place of "sheer silence"; where we once again "hear" the voice of God say, "pick up your cross, and follow me."

I am intrigued by the story of Elijah's "meltdown" recorded in 1 Kings 19 where after his battle with the prophets of Baal he flees to a remote part of the country for fear of his life. There in a time of depression and exhaustion he questions his very existence. God comes to him in the "sheer silence" and reminds him that he is not the only faithful one in Israel, but also asks why is out in the desert. The story as it is relayed in Scripture does not appear to be sympathetic to Elijah and his state, but rather tells of God giving him his next task as a prophet. There is a sense that now Elijah has "heard" God's voice he is to get back to the calling that God had placed upon his life. Perhaps expressed in New Testament terms, "pick up your cross and follow me."

The lesson I am also learning is that this faith journey is best taken in community. BJ has been an inspiration in this regard. She intentionally gathered family and friends around her for her journey. The interplay of the singular and plural in Bible verses such as 1 Peter 2:4–5 and Romans 12:1–2 point to the biblical design of community, not individualism.

> Come to him, a living stone, though rejected by mortals yet chosen and precious in God's sight, and *like living stones, let yourselves be built into a spiritual house.* (1 Pet 2:4–5 NRSV, emphasis mine)

That is to say, we as individual stones (plural) are to be built into a spiritual house (singular).

Faith Reflections

> I appeal to you therefore, brothers and sisters, by the mercies of God, to *present your bodies as a living sacrifice.* (Rom 12:1 NRSV, emphasis mine)

Similarly, our bodies (plural) presented as a living sacrifice (singular). Perhaps this is one of the biggest rewards, and yet challenges, we have; to respond to God's call to live in community and so love God with our whole being and our neighbours as ourselves.

Selwyn Hughes expresses this from personal experience in his biography. His wife was in hospital undergoing surgery for stomach cancer at a time when he was presenting a "Caring" seminar as part of his ministry. He asked the audience to imagine that they were sitting next to him in church and he had opened up to them about his critically ill wife. What would they do with him?

> People began to shout out Scripture texts, but I said, "No, I don't want them now." There was a hushed silence. People seemed nonplussed at the fact that as a Bible teacher I rejected the idea of giving me texts. I explained, "Anyone can give Scriptures to people and there is time and place for that, but what I need this moment is something different—not a succession of texts but the knowledge that someone cares." They quickly got the point. Some in the audience starting shouting out things like, "We love you Selwyn." And "Come down from the platform and let us give you a hug." . . . [A] rather tall man ran down the aisle from the back of the hall, leapt up on the platform and gave me one of the biggest hugs I have received in my life. After he had returned to his seat I said, "Now I feel cared for!"[6]

The ministry of encouragement cannot be done in isolation and is always wrapped in flesh and blood and tangible action. BJ's last sermon on the ministry of encouragement in the life of Mary and Elizabeth come to mind.

So my focus turns to the future—a future that is bright and wholesome and energised by the love of a redemptive God. I am learning to live with the loss of our beautiful daughter and the open-endedness of this journey. I am also learning to celebrate her amazing legacy and the beautiful ways in which she has impacted my life, the life of my family and many others. Yes, I am still learning—this is an expression of the mystery and

---

6. Selwyn Hughes, *My Story: From Welsh Mining Village to Worldwide Ministry*, extended ed. (Surrey: CWR, 2007), 312.

open-endedness of the journey on which God has invited me. I am grateful for a community of family, friends and church that, in those moments of darkness and despair, have embraced me as a tangible expression of God's redemptive love. The journey continues!

One of the ways BJ's story of hope is being retold is through the BJ Foundation for Missions. This foundation supports young people in short- and long-term mission experiences. It was BJ's conviction that as young people move out of their comfort zones and into new experiences in serving others, God's voice will be heard in the "sheer silence."

May many more hear God's call to serve God and others "under his sky"!

www.ingramcontent.com/pod-product-compliance
Lightning Source LLC
Chambersburg PA
CBHW050832160426
43192CB00010B/1995